For a happier & lower stress job, relationships and life!

Unraveling the Mystery of People

(Regardless of who they are and where they're from!)

JAYNE –

I HOPE YOU FIND VALUE

& ENJOYMENT WITH THIS BOOK!

James "Jay" Hawreluk

ISBN: 978-1-936417-46-9

Published by PCG Business, a division of Pilot Communications Group, Inc. 317 Appaloosa Trail Waco, TX 76712

HOW TO REACH THE AUTHOR:

www.JayHaw.com

DEDICATION

This book is dedicated to everyone mentioned in the stories (especially my wife, Jeannie) for without them, this book would not be possible for as we all know, truth is always funnier and better than fiction — especially when dealing with those things called people!

PURPOSE OF THIS BOOK

The purpose of this book is for you to better understand how you are wired. Once you better understand you, you will understand the environment in which you best thrive at work to improve your current status or even find more satisfying employment; deal with people on a more objective basis knowing how they are wired; enhance your relationships; eliminate the minor people issues and improve overall life satisfaction!

CONTENTS

SECTION I:

WHAT'S GOING ON?

CHAPTER #1

An Introduction

Wouldn't a starting salary of $420,000 with lots of perks and benefits be amazingly FANTASTIC for most of us?

What IF ... you like to work with other people BUT were required to sit behind a desk, alone in a cubicle and crunch numbers all day long?

What IF ... you wanted to be part of the decision making process BUT had to ask permission to do absolutely anything?

What IF ... you like working autonomously, but your boss micromanaged every one of your assignments?

Despite the outrageous pay, the job would start to take its toll after a while. Stress levels would continue to increase as you had to change who you are every day to do the job. After a while, the money would not seem so great as the job would become drudgery. Each day it would be harder and harder to get out of bed and go to work; each day would bring more displeasure with the work environment; each day you would become more stressed and irritable; each day you would have less positive personal interactions as people would want to avoid you!

Yet that is what many people do on a daily basis and don't get paid $420,000 for it!

Why would someone dislike such a great-paying job? The answer is in the fact that the wiring requirements of this job are the exact opposite of the person's personal hardwiring. Not only would the jobs be hard to do, but the propensity for success would be very low.

Here is the principle: When your environment matches your innate hardwiring, the odds of succeeding are greatly improved. This applies whether you are an employee of an organization, a manager, a CEO or a budding entrepreneur.

But there's more:

When you understand your hardwiring and the hardwiring of others — at work, in personal relationships, with just plain dealing with other people!

We'll explain hardwiring a little later, but how you are wired determines the environment you best thrive within and how you innately wish to have your ideas implemented, how you communicate, accept pressure and make decisions!

This book is filled with personal, real life stories to help develop each of the concepts. We talk here about how job stress can negatively impact a person and their relationships. My daughter-in-law, Melanie had a phenomenal paying position — she made very good income, great job perks, won trips — sounds like the job of a lifetime! However, Melanie would come home from work and vent about her day.

Why vent so much with this great position? The reason is that Melanie had to change her natural self or wiring every day to be successful at her position. This change created stress. Over time, the stress increased and the "fun" of the job decreased. Gradually, Melanie would come home "stressed out" venting about her day. Her husband, my step-son Craig, at first accepted the venting as her way of relieving stress. The more Melanie "vented" the more Craig began to look at her venting as hostility and aggression — which by his wiring he did not like. Rather than face Melanie's venting, Craig decided not to be home when she came home. He instead would go fishing with his buddy — not aggression, no conflict, just fishing with a friend.

The more Melanie exhibited her stress, the more Craig would go fishing. One night a week of fishing turned into five nights a week of fishing. Melanie was just venting, Melanie thought. Craig was just seeking peace and calm. However, Craig viewed Melanie's venting as too much aggression and wanted a less conflict filled environment. Melanie could not understand why Craig was gone so much. Their relationship started to deteriorate.

One day, Melanie called to discuss their situation. Sitting down with them, understanding how they were wired and reacted to situations enabled them to understand the "whys" of what each were doing. Once they both understood how they were wired and their unique channels, the mystery of what they did and why they did it went away! Today, I'm happy to say, their marriage is stronger than ever and we have two wonderful grandsons!

How you are wired determines the environment you best thrive within.

The point is that when we have to be who we are not, stress occurs that can impact our job performance, our personal relationships and even our own happiness.

Square peg, square hole

Over the years, I've had the pleasure and honor of working with more than 100 different companies and speaking to thousands of individuals, helping them solve some of their "people problems."

The assessing and training that I have done contains some elements that absolutely don't make sense right away, but when the individuals eventually figure out how it works and why, and the benefits that come from that understanding, you should see the lights come on!

Do you wonder when someone says something, you just don't get them?

Do you wonder how anyone could take a huge risk in decision making without doing all of the research?

Do you wonder why some relationships start out so easy, but end up so complicated?

All of the above questions are the results of your hard-wiring. Once you understand how you are wired and others are wired, the mysteries go away.

The end result is tremendous to see!

It's all about figuring out how we think, how we reason, and why. There are more than 250 behavioral assessment tools out there in the marketplace, and I'm familiar with a good portion of them, and they all measure different things, but the best personality assessments that I have ever found are the ones that measure your unique hardwiring or channels.

When you discover the channels unique to you — it changes your world. You discover why you do what you do and why others do what they do. **The value and benefit of this understanding is truly limitless!**

When you discover your unique channels you will be able to connect with your friends in a whole new way; improve personal relationships; understand the environment you thrive best within; understand the job fit that matches your wiring; better understand your employer, boss, co-workers and direct reports so you can deliver precisely what each are looking for. The hiring "warm bodies theory" doesn't work. My personal research has shown that if a person has the background, skill set, and drive pattern needed for the position, the propensity for success is 85%. If they have the background, and the skill set but the opposite drive pattern, the propensity for success is 15%. Standard hiring without using any other instruments is about a 40% success rate. That means the person hits the ground running, making a positive contribution in the shortest period of time.

If you are someone who has hired people in the past, isn't it frustrating to go through the hiring process with all sorts of candidates, interviewing, checking references and finally making an offer to a candidate only to 90 days later be scratching your head wondering who this person is?

Not long ago I had a client who had between 60-80 sales-people working across the country. I told them how to run each prospective employee through a simple personality assessment. I explained the process and they were ready, but for some reason, they figured they had a better method for selecting new sales-people.

Their process was to just hire anybody who had a sales background. Nine months later, they called and said, "Jay, this isn't working out for us."

I replied, "I'll tell you what, let's take a look at your top 10 salespeople and outline their profiles and use them as a template." They agreed, and after running their top 10 salespeople through a personality assessment, we had a pretty clear picture of who the "ideal" sales rep might be for that specific position.

I then explained, "Only hire these types of people in the next 90 days and let me know what you think."

After 90 days, they called me. They excitedly said, "Wow, our salespeople have really improved a lot!"

The company made a standard profile to hire for all of their salespeople and that year (they are more than a 40-year-old company) they boasted a record sales year, all because they had the right people in the right seats.

When you discover the channels unique to you — it changes your world!

Going a step farther, have you ever applied for your dream job, interviewed and been hired only to really dislike the position a short time later?

Several months ago, a client's son called me to discuss his career and job future. He stated: "You know, I have always enjoyed and been fascinated by the law. During law school, I was struggling in which direction I wanted to take. On the suggestion of my dad, I decided to become a litigator. I still love law, but I hate litigation."

After looking at his hard wiring, or channels, it became apparent that he really disliked conflict! Litigation is filled with conflict. Right passion, wrong career in the law!

Square peg, round hole

It's easy to see a company not hiring correctly and say, "Yeah, they should know better. What are they thinking?"

But when it comes down to us on a personal level, we are often guilty of the exact same thing. We think we can do a job just because someone else has succeeded at it, and we quickly find out that it isn't so easy.

Again, let's consider a sales position. Why do people take sales positions in the first place? Quite often they think it's easy and that they can make good money ... even if they have no sales experience, no interest in selling, and no idea if they have the right drive pattern for a salesperson. Talk about flying blind!

My buddy is a car salesman and he consistently knocks down $120K-$130K per year selling cars. He's not a manager or an owner. He just sells cars and he is great at it.

I may think to myself, "He is doing so good, making six figures per year. I should do it." The problem is that I'm wired completely opposite of him and I would get so frustrated and stressed that ultimately I would not succeed at that position.

If you have chased a job and paycheck that took you in a direction that seemed all wrong to you, full of stress, drama, and frustration, then it would seem logical that you are going the wrong way. Understand your channels, understand where you best fit.

I don't know about you, but my life has been filled with bad decisions. The list is endless, but here is a short sample:

- Thinking I really understood someone, only to be taken advantage of.
- Unnecessary arguments.
- Relationships gone bad.
- Chasing dreams that weren't even mine.
- Putting pressure and stress on myself.

· Misinterpreting what people said to me.
· Feeling frustrated at work.

Can you relate to any of the above? If you can then you're probably thinking to yourself, "So what! All of those things have happened to me, too. What makes you so special?"

Nothing makes me special. We have all done these same things, some to a greater degree, others less. Right? Being the go-getter that I think I am, I believed that bad decisions were my lot in life. But instead of giving up and just accepting that things were as they were, I kept looking for answers.

I have always considered myself to be a relatively intelligent individual, but my bad decisions seemed to say otherwise. I went to college and received both a Bachelors and a Masters degree in business. After working for others, I decided it was time to go into business for myself. Someone I really thought I knew and trusted made me an offer to become a business partner. I jumped in without hesitation — making a risk decision with very little information or proof.

Do you understand yourself?

And, as it turned out, that was a very bad move. Over time, the partnership dissolved and I operated the business on my own. I would trust customers who did not pay on time or even pay their bills at all. I would hire the "next greatest employee" only to be scratching my head 90 days later trying to figure out why I hired such a non-performer (after all, they had said all the right things in the interview).

During this time period, my relationships also suffered. I would defend my point of view and chase the other person away. When I was given an ultimatum in a relationship, I always chose the you-had-better-not-do-this scenario. Is life supposed to be this way?

Looking back, not only did I not understand others, I didn't understand myself! Talk about confused.

Finally, in 2000, I was introduced to a personality assessment that would change my life forever. It is an assessment that measures an individual's unique wiring or channels. The concept is that people are wired in a unique way since birth. Their wiring determines how they interact with people.

I began to understand other people and more importantly, I actually began to understand myself! It was my big "Ah-Ha" moment.

Over the next 10 years of my career as a Consultant, I helped thousands of people understand the environment they best thrived within, help them to understand how others are put together, improved working relationships and even helped in personal relationships with their significant other, their children and parents!

It wasn't long before my clients starting asking for reading material that they could use to better understand themselves and their business and personal relationships.

That is how this book came to be. My hope is that you will use it fully so that you can wisely work with all your relationships, take advantage of every opportunity that comes your way, and save yourself untold pain and stress.

This book is a key to your success.

Contained within the following pages, you will…

1) Better know you and others
2) Resolve issues faster and easier
3) Understand how to improve idea exchange
4) Improve communication
5) Know why some people thrive under pressure and others do not
6) Understand risk in decision making and how this impacts people interactions
7) Know the environment you best thrive within to match jobs that make you energized, not stressed

And most importantly take the mystery away from why people do the things that they do — for good!

CHAPTER #2

Why?

You have probably heard the phrase, "If you have a strong enough WHY, the HOW will take care of itself." The point is, of course, that we are motivated to take action when we have a very strong reason to do so.

When it comes to understanding personalities, the same core principle applies. Here, our WHY is still a strong motivator — it makes us get up and go — but it also dictates WHAT we will do. Oftentimes "what" we do is done automatically without thinking about it — the true WHY of what we do creates the mystery of dealing with others; whether or not they are wired like us or very differently.

I have found that once I understand the "why" factors of a person, then the mystery of what they actually do goes away. It makes sense.

I'll explain this further as we explore four important aspects to each of our hardwiring or channels:

#1 — Dominance Channel

Have you ever wondered to yourself, or even asked:

· Why don't you ever let me have control over anything?
· Why are my ideas so good and your ideas are so bad?
· Why is a good head-banging argument fun for some
   people, but complete agony for others?

The above statements are all questions we have asked about other people over the years. My wife and I have been together for more than 20 years. We have had many good times and many bad times, just like every married couple. One thing that used to plague our relationship was the discussion of ideas. She always had the best way of doing things and I always had the best way of doing things. Or, in other words, I would never accept her ideas and she would never see the brilliance of mine!

As you can image, we would draw a line in the sand and dare each other to cross it. Both of us kind of liked the head-banging, argue it out, approach, but after a while it was becoming old for both of us to continue with the "line in the sand" approach to dealing with each other.

Things really came to a head one Thanksgiving weekend. We had one of our fights in front of the squirrels, birds, neighbors — just about every living being that was in ear shot of our voices. The reason for our big drag-out fight was the mere idea of how to construct a pigeon cage. This "truly meaningful" fight almost cost us our marriage.

Three months earlier, my wife, Jeannie, came home from work to find a pigeon severely wounded on our front porch. "Pidg," as we grew to call the bird, had a broken wing and broken leg from being hit by a car. Mother Nature (as my wife's family likes to call her) immediately came to the rescue. After all, we all know there are just not enough pigeons in the world!

She informed me that she was going to take an old laundry basket and fix up a veterinary ward in the garage to nurse the poor pigeon back to health. Several months went by and the pigeon did improve. The leg healed, but the wing was slow to mend.

That Thanksgiving weekend my wife asked me to build a cage so the pigeon would have more room and better facilities in our garage as the cold winter approached. I agreed and went to the building supply store to get the necessary wood and screen to build the cage.

I will tell you that my wife is someone who likes her ideas best and will fight for them … and I am someone who likes my ideas best and will fight for them. You can probably guess her reaction when she entered the garage and saw me constructing the pigeon cage "my way."

"What are you doing?" she asked. "Building the pigeon cage you wanted," was my reply. "But why that way?" she said. "I know it's not the way you wanted it, but my way is better!" She didn't think so and the exchange continued until it transformed into a huge fight; but I must also say that it was the last big fight we ever had.

Using the language of personality assessments, we are all innately wired to be High or Low Dominance, with natural variations in between. If you challenge High Dominance people on an idea or concept that they want, that person will challenge you right back. Why? Because they accept challenge and conflict and give that back to others. My wife and I are both wired to be High Dominance people and thus have the best ways of doing something — the best ideas! And since we both accept challenge and will defend our ideas, well you get why we fought!

Not understanding "why" the person does this can create never-ending arguments or chase the other person away. If one High Dominance person is challenged by another High Dominance person, then the two (both accepting challenge and conflict) will continue to press their points of view. The back and forth continues, but no real resolution or agreement occurs.

We tend to give to others the things we innately need ourselves.

Low Dominance people are a different story. If they are challenged to defend their point of view by a High Dominance individual, the conflict is uncomfortable for every Low Dominance person. They hate it. The confrontation is painful, and many will simply walk away. The High dominance person therefore concludes that everyone else, because they chose not to defend their point of view, has ideas that are not very good.

The "why" here is that High Dominance people challenge others because they expect to be challenged themselves! The Low Dominance individuals, on the other hand, don't feel that arguing is necessary to accomplish a task.

Can you be both right and wrong at the same time?

Can they both be right? Yes and no, it all depends upon their channels to develop their perspective.

More on this in chapters 5 and 6 that cover High Dominance (Dominators) and Lower Dominance (Accommodators).

#2 — Communication Channel

Have you ever relayed a thought to someone and then that person just stare blankly back at you? Have you had people talking to you who keep talking and talking and talking and never allow you time to think?

Perhaps you have wondered:

- Why does the blank stare bug me so much? Can I trust them? What is going on in their mind? Why do they seem so secretive?
- Why does no response cause me to continue to verbalize? (Maybe they just didn't hear me and I have to repeat myself — and in volume!)
- Why do you go off to Neverland while I keep talking? Are the lights on, but nobody is home? Are you off in your own little world?

Can you relate to these scenarios? Or maybe you have been on the receiving end of these scenarios?

I began to see the great differences in communication when I owned my own business. My income and the income of those I employed was dependent upon generating income into the business, which meant I was in sales. I never really wanted to be a salesperson, but being a fairly friendly person, I figured sales would be easy. After all, I reasoned, you just relay your message, solve a problem for the customer, and the order would be yours. Right! Wrong!

As you can imagine, I learned the hard way that selling is not quite that easy. In an effort to increase sales, I started exploring different types of sales techniques. I had heard from somewhere that the person who speaks first has lost. This was very accurate in the sales closing process. It seemed that whoever made the first verbal response was not going to get what they wanted. If the customer did not want to be sold and spoke first, the salesperson would win. And, unfortunately, vise versa.

I would prepare for my sales presentations, solve a need for the customer, ask small closing questions to lead to the final decision, and then ask the final closing question for the order.

Silence.

Dead silence from the prospect.

The blank stare was killing me!

Someone had to say something, and I did. I didn't close many sales in the early days. That same blank stare would haunt me at home. I would tell my wife extremely interesting, edge-of-your-seat stories that were not only humorous, but informative. In the middle of these stories I could sense my wife was in front of me physically but had gone away mentally.

Understanding what drives you crazy ... will help you not drive others crazy!

When she zoned back into the real world, I would ask her how the atmosphere was on Pluto that day. Although stated in the form of a jest, it really did irritate me. One day, I finally asked her why she would "go away" while I was talking. (Yes, she did think that I talked too much!) She explained that as I spoke, she needed time to think her answer through before responding. It wasn't personal, just that my continual verbalization interfered with her thoughts and her ability to provide a response. She needed time to absorb what I was saying.

The light bulb went off! She wasn't ignoring me, being mean, or acting aloof. She simply needed me to be quiet for a minute.

She is an Internal Thinker; I am an External Thinker! I suddenly realized that my customers who gave me the blank stare also needed time to process. I learned to apply this reality to my sales presentation, and now I close a lot of sales.

#3 — Pressure Channel

Have you ever asked:

· Why do some of us like following a plan and find it so hard to deviate?
· Why do I make a list of priorities, but start wherever I want and others make a list and actually stick to that order?
· Why do some of us put pressure on ourselves and we actually work better?
· Why does pressure cause others to perform slower?

Following a plan and dealing with pressure don't seem to go hand in hand at first glance, but for many of us, they actually do go together quite well. My stepdaughter, Angie, and her husband, Ed, both enjoy following a plan. Several years ago, Angie called and said that she and Ed were going to stop by our house after they ran several errands. It was 2 p.m. when she called, and we were expecting them at 5 p.m. for dinner.

They showed up at 5:45 p.m. They did call and let us know they would be running late, but it still frustrated my wife and me. When they finally arrived, Angie would say that things just did not go according to the plan, there were a few snags along the way, and that they just had to finish what they set out to do.

I suggested that they should just change their plans so that they could be on time. Angie looked astonished. She replied, "I really can't relax until we run every errand, and in the proper order. Changing the plan at the last minute creates pressure, but following the plan brings satisfaction to me and Ed."

My wife and I would scratch our heads, not understanding this at all. I admit that I was thinking, "Who cares about the order or about doing every errand? Just be here on time! Do your errands earlier or later, but top priority is being where you say you'll be."

This scenario happened several times over the years. I give Angie and Ed credit for trying to plan extra time so they could arrive on time, and sometimes they did. Those were the times that the plan went according to plan! Other times, it didn't work out, and they arrived late. My wife and I adjusted by making sure that dinner was served at least an hour after they were scheduled to arrive, but we still did not understand why following the plan was just so important to them.

Now we do understand.

#4 — Decision Making Channel

Have you ever wondered or asked:

· Why are the bullet points not enough information for some?
· Why do some people need and relay lots and lots of details?
· Why are other people so set on structure and the rules when you think they are just basic guidelines that can be changed?

Those who crave a lot of information and detail are the same people who crave for rules, regulations, and structure.

As varying and different as communication is, so is the exchange of information. No doubt you know people who give a lot of details and others who just don't give enough. You need to know that each person feels that he or she is giving you the appropriate amount of information, but it may be way too much or way too little for you.

When I was running my own company, I had two separate discussions, one with our salesperson and the other with our operations scheduler. They had both gone on a sales appointment with an important client and met with me individually to discuss the specifics of that appointment. The operations scheduler was first. He came into my office and proceeded to relay the following information:

We arrived at the sales appointment seven minutes early so we would be on time. When we arrived, we were greeted by the receptionist who told us the person we would be meeting with would be ready in five minutes. Well, it wasn't five minutes; it was almost fifteen minutes.

After walking us down the hall, we were seated in the conference room. We presented our ideas and answered the client's questions concerning production time, delivery, and terms. After an hour and twenty minutes, the prospective client agreed to our proposal and we secured the sale.

It was frustrating to me because the sales person ignored our company rule of not extending terms over 30 days without approval and granted 45-day terms. Everything else went well, with the exception of the terms, and that really does bug me.

The operations scheduler left and the salesperson then came into my office. I asked how the appointment went, and he replied:

Went really well and we got the sale.

That was a short summary, even for me, so I asked, "Anything else?"

Oh, yeah, we need to give them 45-day terms.

The funny thing is that both of them thought they had relayed the exact same story, with the exact same amount of information and detail. And in reality, they actually had!

Adding up the differences

You are wired one way, and you want people to be sensitive to your uniqueness, right? I do as well, and what that means is that we must be sensitive to the differences in the way other people are wired. It's the WHY behind their actions, because the way they are wired determines how they will act.

When we understand how other people react to Dominance, Communication, Pressure, and Decision Making, it will make all the difference in the world. I guarantee that it will bring you new clarity in dealing with those around you.

All of a sudden what people say and how they say it will resonate with their specific hardwiring — their specific channels — and it will take the mystery away!

CHAPTER #3

Behavior Is So Baffling

People have been trying to figure each other out since the beginning of time, and I'm not sure we have made all that much progress. Sure, there are thousands of books about behavior and understanding human behavior out there, but every generation seems to start at the same point, ask the exact same questions, and make the same mistakes.

What complicates or confuses things (depending on which way you look at it) is the fact that behavior is made up of both internal and external elements. These two sets of elements, as varied as they are, across all cultures, countries, and traditions, affect every single one of us. There is no escaping it.

Therefore, to really understand people, it is important to look at these two elements.

The key point is that people are confusing because of their behavior. The person we see — their behavior — is made up of all sorts of elements coming internally and externally. Once we remove the "behavior" of an individual and understand their hardwiring, the mystery of what they do and why they do it disappears and we better understand ourselves and others!

The Internal Elements

The internal elements that affect you are usually things that you are born with. You can't help it, and it often can't be trained out of you. It's just the way you are.

Understanding the following three parts will give you a very clear picture of what's innately inside of you, and everyone else:

#1: Hardwiring

People are basically hardwired to do things in a certain way. Their hardwiring is mentally genetic, which simply means that they are born that way. Each person has their own unique combination of four distinct channels which make up their hardwiring. Those four channels we briefly discussed in the last chapter:

1) Dominance channel,
2) Communication channel,
3) Pressure channel, and
4) Decision-making channel.

Everyone has a high degree or low degree of each of these channels. Mathematically, these four options produce many, many possible combinations, so it is no wonder that we feel confused by all the differences we see in other people.

Understanding how people are hardwired will allow you to cut through "behavioral" issues and understand the WHY behind them. (Why people do the things they do including why I do the things I do!) Once you know your why, you can better understand you and the impact you have on others. Once you understand their why, you can better understand their actions and the impact they have on you and others. Since this revelation also applies to you on a personal level, you can, as a direct result, improve your-self, your interpersonal relationships and the results you achieve from dealing with other people in all aspects of your life. Thus, this is the purpose and point of this book!

However, to fully understand these channels, you must continue to explore all of the behavioral items that affect each person and to some degree cloud their hardwiring.

At the end of this book — Chapter 18 — you will have the opportunity to assess your channels and the channels of other people.

#2: Intelligence

Intelligence is a very strong factor in creating someone's overall persona or behavior. That is why we assume, based upon a chosen vocation or stated interest, that we know what someone's behavior will be.

Is this accurate? Sure, there are stereotypical examples that fit every mold, but using a stereotype is not really fair, is it? The phrase, "assumption is the lowest form of knowledge," would certainly apply here.

Let's look at an example. Think about medical doctors. I've had the pleasure of working with many physicians and found that most of them are very pleasant, very nice individuals. However, a lot of people think that physicians are arrogant and base that assumption on the doctors' high level of intelligence.

But think about it. If we all operate in four different channels, it would be accurate to recognize that there is going to be a wide range of variation between doctors. To assume that a lot of schooling means you will be arrogant is equal to assuming that no schooling will make you humble. The point is, a stereotype fits a very small percentage of the population, and it is therefore inaccurate to apply that to the rest of the world.

Intelligence may affect how well you speak or think, but it does not change your natural channels.

Intelligence is not only related to schooling, though these days we do look at degrees, titles, and awards as a measure of intelligence. With all that said, your innate intelligence does affect your persona and behavior, and it is an important factor to consider. But regardless of intelligence, their channels are their channels!

#3: Skill Set

Our natural skill sets (innate abilities) will also affect our behavior. These skill sets may be our ability to perform as musicians, create art, be adept in business, play sports, program computers, etc. The list goes on and on.

Let me provide you with a great example. My physical stature is fairly medium for a male: 5'8" tall, medium style build. This is my physical appearance, and my hard-wiring and channels would be the same in me whether I was good at sports or not.

Your natural skill is you, regardless of how much money you make.

But, let's say that at my 5'8" height I could sink a 3-point shot from 40 feet away with 75% accuracy while being guarded by a 7-foot basketball player. Would that be a great skill set? Sure!

With that ability, I would probably be playing in the NBA. And if that were the case, would my behavior be different if I were making $10 million a year, wearing plenty of bling, and hanging out with my posse? Definitely! But understand this: my channels would still be the same.

Your natural skill is you, regardless of how much money you make, the deals you sign, or the good or bad bounces you get in life. Skill set may impact behavior, but their wiring channels are their channels! And someone's channels can definitely explain the role they play on their team, the pressure they accept, the decisions they make and who wants the ball at the end of the game!

The External Elements

We have outlined the three internal elements that are innately you. Now we are going to focus on the three external elements that, through outside forces, have an affect on you.

#1: Upbringing

One of the strongest influences on our behavior is our upbringing. We have needs as children that can change our behaviors, in addition to the influences we receive from the adults in our life as we grow up.

According to the philosopher John Locke — who coined the term "nurture" — which represented the view that humans acquire all or almost all their behavioral traits from environmental influences, such as upbringing.

The behavioral changes can actually work against our natural channels and this can create high levels of stress. With my particular channel pattern, I am someone who enjoys and needs a lot of external validation from others. This is true today and was true when I was growing up.

My father was rather disconnected from my siblings and me while we were growing up. As a matter of fact, on my 18th birthday, my dad informed me that he was glad I was finally a man because he could never "get" nor "deal" with children. This was a shock to me, but it did explain an awful lot about our interaction when I was growing up.

As someone who needs external validation from others, I sure didn't get any from him. All of my external validations came from my mother. As I did things she liked, I received positive validations from her, and of course the reverse was also true. For years I would try to emulate my mom's behavior in order to receive positive validation.

The many years of trying to suppress who I actually am in order to receive the positive validation from my mom that I wanted created high levels of stress. This stress caused me to have a severe bleeding ulcer at the age of 15!

The doctors were completely confused at the time. How could a 15-year-old be under so much stress that it created a bleeding peptic ulcer? I didn't understand it either, but when I became a consultant and began investigating a person's channels, it made good sense. My mom's channels are the exact opposite of mine!

So you can see that trying to change my behavior and working against my channels, all to get the positive validation I needed, created massive amounts of stress in my life. It turns out that stress can affect people physically, emotionally and mentally. When individuals *(If you are a parent, this really applies to you!)* are aware of their own channels and the channels of those around them, and work accordingly, stress will decrease substantially.

Even today, people will say how much I behave like my mom. The difference today is that I understand myself and work with my channels, not against them.

#2: Life's Experiences

Life's experiences are a strong influence on our behavior. This includes our education we receive, our good and bad experiences, and our failures and successes at work and in our personal lives. It all can affect our external persona or behavior.

I am a particularly trusting person. I believe what people tell me and don't feel compelled to check them out or verify their statements (Sound familiar to many of you?).

It is my nature to trust people, and yes, I've been taken to the cleaners! But that's who I am.

Today, because I've shown trust and been taken advantage of so many times, I am not as trusting as I once was. My behavior has changed, but my channels are still the same.

These channels are what created my innate trust in people and those channels are why I was so trusting of others and why I never did my homework. I sure could have saved a lot of time, headaches and money if I had only known this when I was 21 years old!

My life experiences have tempered my behavior. It's natural for me to trust other people, but now I also do my homework.

#3: Gender

Gender has always confounded us when it comes to behavior. The men are from one side of the universe and the women from the other. Gender will create certain common behaviors. If you think about it simply, women are biologically designed to be nurturers and thus conversation and actions will be driven by that biology — family, home, emotional items. Men are biologically designed to be the providers and their conversations and actions are driven as such — sports, games, physical items.

Stop trying to figure out behavior by gender and start understanding how "the person" is wired.

#4: Race, Culture, Religion

I had the privilege of doing a presentation at Lehigh University for their Global Village project. The Global Village is a six week business program that encourages young students and leaders from around the world to grow in their business and leadership abilities through intensive work with a cross cultural and global team. This better prepares them for the global economy.

The group I presented to was comprised of 100 students from 52 different countries around the world. Talk about a mix of race, culture, gender and religion. Once we looked past how they "behaved" and looked at how they were wired, people could easily understand each other. You see, wiring patterns are across the board and not affected by race, gender, culture or religion.

Regardless of race, there was a mixture of wirings. There were just as many females wired like males in the audience. Although culture and religion created differing behaviors of the attendees, wiring patterns were clearly defined in each individual. Once clearly defined to the audience, every person had a common language in which to interact — by their unique channels determined by their hardwiring!

The conclusion is that we can understand people better — regardless of where they come from — by understanding how people are wired and their unique channels.

#5: Miscellaneous

In addition to our upbringing and life experiences, there are all sorts of miscellaneous factors that make up our overall behavior. These can include your birth order, your maturity level, your friends, your teachers, and so on. Any of these can positively or negatively affect your behavior.

I am the oldest of my siblings, and my brother and sister are fraternal twins. The reason my brother happens to be the middle child is that he happened to say "hello" to the world minutes before my sister did.

What is interesting about Chris is that he suffered from "middle child" syndrome for many years of his life. To hear him tell the story of growing up, he'll say he was fed in the garage with the dog, that he was forced to sleep in the attic, or that the only clothes he got were discards from my sister or me.

He was convinced that I received all of the special privileges because I was the oldest and that our sister received preferential treatment because she was the youngest and the only girl.

While the above story is an exaggeration, the real deal is that we three grew up in a very average family (not sure what a "normal" family is — we'll save that for another book). My brother ate with the rest of the family in the kitchen, he slept in a bed in a bedroom (my brother and I shared a bedroom growing up), and he actually had clothes bought for him. For some reason, and I never knew why, he had "middle child" syndrome his entire life.

Do you know your own dominant channel?

Years later, when I understood his channels, everything made sense. As a child, Chris believed that he could do what he wanted to do (which got him in a lot of trouble) and, therefore, he believed he was not treated the same. However, as a High Dominance person, he did not know why he did what he did, so Chris used the "middle child" excuse whenever things did not go his way. As a Bullet Pointer, he drew only upon the information he wanted to use; so his decisions were always right. He didn't need any data or proof to make a decision. Thus, how he was wired created the conclusion in his mind that as the middle child, he got nothing!

Knowing his channels — how he is hard wired — everything he has done now makes sense. Even today I "get" why he says what he says. It doesn't make it right or even believable, but it does make sense.

The reality is that even though I did not understand my brother when we were growing up, his wiring — how he is put together — has contributed to him being very successful as a sales person. He wouldn't take "no" for an answer growing up, made decisions about things on the spot, viewed everything as a personal challenge — while frustrating at times for my parents and others these are all the attributes that have made him successful in sales today!

The point is that we cannot always judge someone by how they act or behave. There are many, many elements that can affect and change our behavior. When you understand what peoples specific channels are, it will give you clarity in how to best interact with them

Understanding the Channels that Create Hardwiring

As you can see, there are numerous elements acting on each one of us from the inside and from the outside, and all of it affects our behavior. I say "affect" because it does indeed affect our behavior, not "cause" our behavior.

Our unique hardwiring that determines our channels are the same way. They do not necessarily equal behavior, but understanding our channels will help us see past people's behavior and find out what makes them tick.

Here are some real examples:

- Jim likes his ideas best and will defend them to the death. Why?
- Theresa is frustrated by the blank stares she gets from people when she is talking. Why?
- Sue can't stay seated for long periods of time. Why?
- Dave gets lost when given complex answers to his basic questions. Why?
- Jim is a High Dominance person and innately likes his ideas and ways of doing things best!

· Theresa is an External Thinker and needs response. Blank stares come from Internal Thinkers!
· Sue is a Pressure Acceptor which creates a more impatient and antsy person!
· Dave is a Bullet Pointer. Too much information makes his head spin!

The important questions that each one of us must learn to ask are these:

#1 — How can I maximize my personal strengths and minimize my limitations?

#2 — How can I better communicate and better observe those around me?

#3 — How can I understand some of the things that happen to me and learn to look at things in a slightly different light?

We are all a mixture of all four channels ... which creates countless combinations!

I've learned to apply these important questions to my own life, and so must you. It's all about learning how you are hard-wired; your particular channels that drive you, and why. Taking it a step farther, once you understand your channels, understanding other's channels and what they do and why, takes away the mystery allowing for better interactions!

SECTION II:

HIGH / LOW DOMINANCE CHANNEL

CHAPTER #4

Why Can't We All Just Get Along?

It is entirely natural that we want some degree of control or dominance over our environment. We also have ideas that we want to see included and incorporated into whatever we are doing.

Why is it then that some people always want things done their way (you know who you are) and others are open to the best way of doing things (you know who you are)? The answer (and the reason) is the dominance channel.

You know from the last chapter that we are "hardwired" a certain way. We all are. It's who we are.

The degree of dominance that you want and need in your environment is based on your individual hardwiring. Those who feel they must have their ideas and their way implemented in a given environment are considered the "high dominance" individuals.

Here are a few interesting characteristics of "Dominators" or high dominance people:

- they accept more conflict in defending their way of doing things
- they believe their ideas are brilliant and best
- they accept elements of face-to-face conflict to defend their ideas
- they may even beat down others ideas
- they feel that non-defended ideas are not that good
- they need to have their way
- they'll only accept other's ideas if they can modify or tweak it to their way

On the other end of the spectrum, as you would imagine, are the "low dominance" individuals. Low dominance people want their good ideas implemented as well, but the major difference is that they are open to using the best ideas that are most beneficial to the team.

Low dominance people are "Accommodators" who:

- work well in a team environment
- want all options and ideas discussed
- want a more harmonious environment
- do not consider that every event is a "head banging session"
- do not like face-to-face conflict and therefore will, many times, acquiesce to the Dominators

Here is an interesting twist. Just because Accommodators might agree with a Dominator, it does not necessarily mean that they will go along with an idea. Accommodators are typically more passively aggressive. They will agree with something because they do not want a conflict, but later they will not follow through with the Dominator's way of doing things. For example, in a meeting a Dominator may state that everyone is to do a certain thing and that anyone with an objection should speak up. Nobody says anything, the meeting is over, but lo and behold, the Accommodators have all decided to do something else!

Accommodators may not passively resist the Dominator; they may just do what the Dominator wants. This creates an atmosphere of dissatisfaction and frustration. In the end the Accommodator may just have had enough and leave a job or even a relationship.

This "me" or "we" issue never goes away because we always have Dominators and Accommodators.

Are you a Dominator or an Accommodator?

My wife, for some reason, really loves concrete. We have an older home and in the laundry room we have a huge washtub basin. The thing is huge and it is old. The basin was made in 1948 (it's stamped underneath it), and what's more, it leaks!

One day, we were standing downstairs in the laundry room and she looked at the old basin and said, "I don't know if I should fix that."

Without thinking, I replied, "Yeah, I don't think you can. It's probably too hard of a job."

Well, what did that do? She made it her mission to fix that decrepit basin and she did a great job doing so. Today, it works great, and doesn't leak a bit.

People have asked her, "Does Jay say these things to bug you?"

She tells them, "No, it doesn't bug me. Instead, it motivates me."

Are you an Accommodator?

I must explain that if she didn't think the tub was worth saving, and she didn't want to do it at all, that she would have done nothing. But because it was important to her, she took action.

Now, let me test you: What was my wife really saying when she told me, "I don't think this is fixable"? Before you guess, know that my wife is a Dominator, and a very high Dominator at that.

Did she want me to fix the basin? No.
Did she want me to buy her a new one? No.
Did she want me to commiserate with her? No.

If you were thinking, "She was probably looking for the challenge," then you are right! As a Dominator, she likes to be challenged. And she proved that she could do it by fixing it herself.

Are you a Dominator?

The next two chapters will look deeper into what it means to be a Dominator or an Accommodator. As you know, having a better understanding of those around you will also help you understand yourself. And dominance is one of those highly misunderstood elements.

CHAPTER #5

My Way Is Best!

As we have already discussed, Dominators have an innate desire for dominance that causes them to dominate their environment, value their own ideas, and push to do things their way.

These Dominators are on the high end of the dominance spectrum. (At the other end you have the Accommodators, and they are discussed in the next chapter.)

So, what are you? Are you a Dominator? An Accommodator? Or somewhere in the middle? Even if in the middle, you probably have a tendency to lean more one way (Dominator) or another (Accommodator).

Understanding Dominators a bit more

Dominators feel that their ways and ideas are the best. That's how they think, and on top of it, they are willing to debate endlessly (or even fight in a personal relationship) to prove it! Let me explain.

Suppose I'm working with Norm to come up with an idea that helps my company work better. We are both Dominators, but it's my company. After I present how my idea best benefits the organization, do you think he'll go for it? Yes, he probably will, but he might modify my idea just a little. Why? Because he is a Dominator and wants things his way.

That doesn't mean that all Dominators are going to hold on to their ideas until the dear end. They are not obstinate, but they do like their ideas best. But depending upon how important their idea is to them, they may hold onto it for a long time — which can appear to be very obstinate to others.

Now, suppose Norm presents an idea and a challenge to me, a fellow Dominator, and I push back a bit, trying to see why his idea is better than mine, and he suddenly backs down. Why would he do that? Does he believe that his idea is valuable? No, he doesn't, because Dominators will fight for whatever they believe in, and if he's not fighting for it, then he doesn't believe in it.

A meeting of Dominators would, as you can imagine, consist of a lot of head butting, arguing, and loud discussions, followed by everyone going out and having a beer together. That would count as a "good meeting" in their books.

Interestingly, Dominators get their self-confidence internally — from themselves, their ideas, their results. So in order to motivate them, you need to give them opportunities to come up with ideas and let them execute those ideas. They need to internalize their ideas on their own and that provides them with self-confidence.

Dominators take note ...

Whether or not we are wired to dominate our environment, we need to express our ideas and have our way at some point. That's a need that applies to everyone, at every age and at every level — regardless of our hardwiring!

Consistently being suppressed or being overly accommodating to the wishes of others will create an emotional buildup that can result in a highly uncharacteristic outburst of rage. Even the most obliging person has a boiling point. When reached, it can produce a needless and ugly confrontation.

A good friend of mine relayed the following story of what happens when an Accommodator finally reaches the point where they are not going to acquiesce anymore! He was married and had a very accommodating daughter — Cathy — who always acquiesced to everyone. She was so nice, so accommodating — no one could say a bad word about Cathy! My friend's sister, Cathy's aunt, was a Dominator, a woman who insisted she knew the best way to get things done and would impose her ideas and agendas on everyone around her. Many times, even if she disagreed, Cathy would go along with whatever her aunt wanted. "It's easier that way," Cathy insisted. "It eliminates conflict."

Because Dominators like their own ideas the best, they accept the element of conflict.

She continued to be the capitulating niece for many years, but when Cathy was about to get married, all hell broke loose. Her aunt stepped in with what she considered to be an "ideal" wedding plan, and Cathy went ballistic. She drove to her aunt's house and exploded, unleashing 15 years of pent up resentment and fury. It was an ugly scene, to say the least.

"Why?" my friend asked her. "This is so uncharacteristic of you."

She replied, apologetically, "I couldn't take it anymore. I do enjoy accommodating others, but I have ideas, too! Once in a while I need to do things my way."

Cathy is not alone, of course, and people in every family, every city, and every country share her plight. Anywhere that dominance and acquiescence routinely collide, this will be an issue. This should serve as a warning to husbands and wives, parents and children, pastors and congregations, employers and employees, CEOs and board members, coaches and players, etc.

Basically, whenever two or more people are working together on something, they need to be aware of this reality.

While visiting a large business several years ago, I conducted a survey and found that over 80% of the employees preferred their own ideas and felt confident that their ways of doing things were superior. I did a bit more research and found that this particular company had a routine 30-minute meeting that would often drag on for hours. Why? Because all those Dominators present would explain and then argue to defend their superior ideas!

Dominators are very tough on themselves as they push hard for results.

As a result of this totally dysfunctional team, projects lumbered to completion well beyond the prescribed deadlines because each person attempted to put his or her own thumb print on the work being done. It was sad and chaotic at the same time.

Where were the Accommodators, the innate team players? They constituted less than 20% of those I surveyed, though they were open to the best ideas, they told me that their voices were rarely heard. They confessed that they found long, contentious meetings to be frustrating and they bemoaned the inability of most of their fellow employees to function as a team.

One man went so far as to say, "I really am open to good ideas, no matter who gives them or where they come from, and I dislike a lot of conflict in the workplace. But when I make a point, I do expect others to listen to me, just as I am prepared to listen to them. That doesn't happen around here, I'm afraid."

"What have you done to correct the situation?" I asked him.

He replied, "Well, to temper the conflict, I mostly agree with what everyone else around the table says. Then I walk out the door and do what I want to do."

"Wouldn't you consider that somewhat passive aggressive?" I asked him.

He nodded and replied, "It sure beats arguing endlessly, but one day I'm going to let this entire dysfunctional team have a piece of my mind."

If he ever did blow up, it would be too late by then to do any good, and as it would seemingly be out of character for him, it would probably not be given much credence.

What's the answer?

The moral of the story is that everyone has ideas that need to be expressed, even if the ideas go unheeded. Over-exposing people to a contentious environment who innately do not like conflict can have disastrous consequences. Suppressing ideas, under the guise of peace and emotional stability, will inevitably take its toll. People who habitually hold back are bound to develop a damaged psyche.

The answer for Dominators is a combination of adding parameters so that their fighting for their idea is profitable to the whole company and giving Accommodators room to speak and present their ideas. This type of atmosphere would have turned this company around, and it will help you in any situation you are in today.

You may not believe me, but I don't fight with my wife any more. We used to draw a line in the sand and have knockdown, drag out, last-man-standing type of fights. It was bad!

Now that we understand each other, we have figured out that we can work together and communicate with each other more effectively. I understand that she likes things her way and she understands that I like my way. We both think that our way is best, but we've learned how to work together.

Here is what we do: If something is her idea and her project, then I can give input, but she has the right to accept or deny my ideas. The same holds true for my projects. This simple approach has brought tremendous peace to our home! This simple approach can be applied by Dominators in all aspects of their lives — personally and professionally to better interact and work together.

CHAPTER #6

The Best Way Is My Way!

It may seem hard to fathom that some people like to argue or that some people actually shrink away from verbal combat. What is pain to one person is pleasure to another!

Wherever you are on the spectrum of Dominance will define what is pain or pleasure for you. It's not right or wrong, it just is. That's the way you have been made.

Understanding how Accommodators think

Accommodators, who have an innate desire to be a team player, will go with the best idea presented. Though they want their ideas to be heard, they aren't going to push it if an even better idea comes to the surface.

Scott is a good example. He's an Accommodator. Suppose he has an idea and I have an idea. I give him information and proof about how my idea best benefits the organization. After I give him some time to think about it, do you think he'll go for my idea? Absolutely! Why? Because Scott is an Accommodator who is innately open to the options that best benefit the team! He is also by nature likely to minimize conflict.

Good managing is giving other people what they need to be successful.

Accommodators look at the world and say, "Not everything is a head-banging event. Not every decision needs to be a heated debate." They look at meetings of Dominators and sigh, saying internally, "What a bunch of jerks and lunatics! They will never get anything done."

For Accommodators, they need to recognize that Dominators are hardwired for dominance. As a result, they are determined to have their way and will passionately defend their ideas. But that's not the end for Accommodators. They must engage, put their own ideas on the table, and work patiently toward the best solution.

That is, after all, what Teamers do best!

Learning to work together

What typically happens in a group or organization is that the idea flow dries up. The Dominators (my way is best, I accept some conflict) are actively aggressive, while the Accommodators (the best way is best, I don't want conflict) are passively aggressive. No matter which way you work it, the Dominator is going to dominate and the Accommodator is going to back off. The Dominator's ideas will rule and the Accommodator's ideas won't even end up on the table.

As this vicious cycle continues, both parties get increasingly frustrated, productivity moves to a standstill, and relationships are strained.

In order to be heard, Accommodators, need to manage their internal reaction to avoid conflict and, at times, need to step it up. Don't take a Dominator's challenge personally. In fact, you need to challenge back. You have a great idea, and you want to follow the best idea, so put yours on the table. If it's chosen, great, and if it's not chosen, then at least you put it out there. I've explained this before to Accommodators and their eyes get really big and they look at me like I've asked them to walk across Niagara Falls on a tightrope. But after they try it, they find that it actually works. They feel better in the process, like they've been heard, and they are better for it. The Dominators, on the other hand, realize that the Teamers also have good ideas that are worth considering.

Additionally, I recommend that Dominators give Accommodators a "conflict free zone" where they are free to express ideas. The Dominators will want to modify an idea a bit to make it their own, and if it's the best idea, Accommodators won't object. When these slightly adjusted ideas become the Dominator's own idea, it becomes important and they will push it through to completion. Sometimes Dominators need to simply allow others to execute their ideas without modification. Other Dominators will appreciate this. And, hey, if Accommodators have to stand up to Dominators at times then the Dominators need to back off the Accommodators!

This win-win scenario is undermined when Accommodators sit back and choose not to engage and when Dominators don't provide room for open idea exchange. From the big things to the little things, this is important.

If I give Norm (a Dominator from the last chapter) a report and he hands it back to me and didn't make any changes on it, how important was it to him? Not important at all! But if he gives it back to me with a few minor changes on it, is that a good thing? Yes it is, because that means he read it and that he put his thumbprint on it.

It's a small detail, but it means a lot!

What you really want is a win-win scenario.

Develop a common language

Not too long ago, when I was doing some work to my office in our house, my wife suggested that I put in a window box. My first response was, "No way!" Because we knew we were both Dominators and had agreed not to jump on each other's ideas or just fight for our own way of doing things, she left it alone.

In this case — after thinking about it for a while — I decided her idea to add the window box to my office wasn't so bad and decided to go with her idea. (I did have to make a minor change or two, since as a Dominator my thumbprint is important on the idea.) As it turns out, it was a great idea and it makes the room so much lighter and brighter.

Our relationship wasn't always that way. Jeannie and I have been together for nearly two decades. We have had many good times and many bad ones, just like almost every couple we know. What has often plagued our relationship was our focus on ideas — hers versus mine, mine versus hers. It seems that she has always thought she knew the best way to do things … and I have always thought I did so too. We were both Dominators, but didn't know it at the time.

We would draw a line in the sand and dare each other to cross it. Both of us seemed to enjoy the head-banging, at least at first, but after a while that line-in-the-sand approach to dealing with one another became really tiresome for each of us.

Since the early days of discovering our hardwiring and learning how to better interact with each other, we have now evolved to a common language.

A key advantage to knowing another person's hardwiring and the specific channels that impact them is being able to cultivate a positive language and positive relationship. What has helped my clientele and, in turn, hundreds and hundreds of managers, employees and those involved in personal relationships has been developing a common language.

Now, when we are working on a project and one of us throws out an idea that the other initially rejects, we'll just say "Turn down your Dominator." These few words relay that the other party needs to listen to the idea instead of bashing it down. This is a non-threatening way to take a step back from something that is a natural response. We get what the other is saying and can achieve a common end result without all of the arguing, fighting or other difficulties that used to haunt our relationship.

When I coach Accommodators on how to better express themselves, it is not unusual for me to say: "Pull up your Dominator side" which is an easy way to say defend your ideas in the face of conflict.

Key Points to Remember:

1) Dominators interacting with Dominators

Dominators by their wiring like their ideas, their plans and their ways of doing things best. Not everything has to be their way, just things that are important to them. When two or more Dominators interact, keep the following in mind:

· Create a general goal, but allow each person control over some particular area of the plan.
· Remember that your way may not be optimal, so be open to the ideas of others. Agree not to just react, but pause before responding as the other idea may just be better!
· Remind people that for full engagement, you need your thumbprint on some aspect of the idea or plan.

2) Dominators interacting with Accommodators

· Dominators: Allow "conflict free" idea exchange with the Accommodators.
· Dominators: Accommodators are just that — accommodating people. However, every person wants to be valued for the specialness that is them, so allow them to contribute and let them have their way whenever possible.
· Accommodators: Stand up for your ideas when you know they are better than anything being imposed upon you. Do not take Dominator conflict personally!

3) *Accommodators interacting with Accommodators*

· The biggest issue with Accommodators dealing with each other is that both want to accommodate the other. For example, two Accommodators deciding what to have for dinner and the conversation may go like this:

"What would you like for dinner?"
"Anything you would like!"
"How about Chinese food?"
"Only if you want Chinese!"
"How about Italian cuisine?"
"Only if Italian works for you!"

You get the idea. The simple solution is to set a time table for the decision; agree to limit to only three options; then vote on the option that works best for all. Note: Sometimes an Accommodator needs to be a bit more domineering to get the group to make a decision.

SECTION III:

EXTERNAL / INTERNAL COMMUNICATION CHANNEL

CHAPTER #7

What Communication Really Is

I am an External Thinker which means to formulate ideas and plans I need to verbalize my thoughts; and as you may be wondering, my wife is the exact opposite. She's an Internal Thinker.

Here is how it looks:

I used to tell her the most interesting, edge-of-your-seat stories that should have kept her captivated ... and in the middle of my conversation I would look up at her and she would be just sitting there physically, but she had zoned out with an expressionless look on her face. My thought was that she had gone away to Pluto.

You know, it's that glazed look in someone's eyes.

I would think to myself, "Why has she gone to Pluto? What did I do? What did I say?" I would get frustrated, even a little hurt, but here is what would happen with her. I would start with my story, and somewhere along the line, I would say something and she would catch on to that statement or little detail and start thinking about it.

Everything else would be blocked out. It was like she had blacked out! She would "come to" a little later, but would have missed my great story.

Now I understand her, and it doesn't frustrate me anymore. She just looks at me and says, "Jay, I've had enough External Thinking time, and I need some Internal Thinking time." I don't take it personally. It makes sense. She thinks/talks one way, and I think/talk another.

Understanding how we think and talk

Did you ever tell a story and get the blank stare back? Do some people keep on talking and talking, not giving you time to think about their question and respond?

How much response do you want from the person you are talking to? That's a very important question. Have you ever thought about that before? Most people haven't.

Do you expect a response from the people you are talking to? On the other hand, you've probably noticed that some people talk out loud until they come up with answers and others think quietly until they come up with the answers. That's why some people are able to come up with good ideas during a meeting, while others have these "revelations" after the meeting is over.

Obviously, everybody talks and everybody thinks. It's how we process the information and how we perform that makes all the difference. The reason humans talk is that we can. It's that simple! However, the key here is how people crystallize thought.

To make it even more meaningful or complicated (depending on how you look at it), the External Thinker gets validation of their thoughts and ideas from response from people important to them. That's why the blank stare actually hurts! For an external thinker, the blank stare is frustrating because what they are saying is not being acknowledged!

Do you get blank stares? Do you give blank stares?

What about you? Do you give the blank stare? Does the blank stare hurt your feelings? Do you think well on the spot or do you need time to process on your own in order to come up with sufficient answers?

Whatever the case, it pays to know.

Dealing with daily life

At work or at home, what usually happens when External Thinkers interact with Internal Thinkers? Here is a common scenario:

Suppose an External Thinker has an argument with an Internal Thinker and the External Thinker says what needs to be said, and then it's done with.

Three days later, the Internal Thinker walks up and says, "I'm mad at you!"

"About what?" the External Thinker asks.

It's obvious to the Internal Thinker. "I've been thinking about what you said and how you said it when we were talking a couple of days ago."

"Uh and when was this?" asks the External Thinker.

Exasperated, the Internal Thinker explains, "On Monday, don't you remember?"

It turns out that the Internal Thinker had stewed over what was said for three days before making a reply. The External Thinker thought the issue had been resolved.

What is really happening?

External Thinkers verbalize out loud to generate ideas and resolve issues, but the Internal Thinkers need to think to generate ideas and resolve issues. Internal Thinkers may talk to people for information, input, etc., but then need time to think to crystallize their decision. They may both come to the same conclusion, but do it differently. And this difference may be a recipe for disaster, anger, hurt, pain, frustration, and miscommunication.

Think of communication in these simple terms:

External Thinkers need to verbalize to crystallize. Internal Thinkers need to internalize to crystallize.

How people process thoughts and ideas is neither right or wrong, it just is! What External Thinkers and Internal Thinkers need to do is to learn how to work together — which will improve communication between the parties.

The External Thinkers need to have some patience with Internal Thinkers. Give them some room to think about a scenario. Saying, "Get back to me when you've had some time to process," is a perfect way to give the Internal Thinker time and freedom to generate a good reply, which is what they want to do anyway.

The Internal Thinkers, on the other hand, should give a response to External Thinkers, even if it's as simple as, "I'll have to get back to you on that." This satisfies the External Thinker's need to be heard and communicated with.

One of my clients is in the hospitality industry with an office manager who is an incredibly Internal Thinker. I mean, VERY internal! She is a fantastic organizer, very attentive to details and runs the property office with a high level of precision.

But, as fate would have it, part of the job of the office manager is to fill in at the front desk. What does this office manager NOT want to do? You guessed it! She does NOT want to talk to people.

So what does she do to get around this obstacle? She hires a lot of External Thinkers for the front desk officer position. Every property under her control has an External Thinker at the front desk. She has effectively created a shield around herself, and she likes it that way.

It comes down to this: communicate!

Knowing yourself and those around can be of great benefit!

CHAPTER #8

I'll Talk Until You Respond!

As socially driven creatures with the ability to talk, we all talk. The interesting point is that some of us actually develop ideas and concepts WHILE we are verbalizing our thoughts. Things come into our heads and we need to verbalize them to generate our best thoughts.

These are the External Thinkers, as we have discussed already, and they need face-to-face interaction with people so they can use their verbal skills to get the response they want, whether that response is positive or negative. External Thinkers think on their feet, they think out loud, and they need to talk all the time.

Annoying? Maybe. But it depends upon how you are hard wired. Right in the middle of a meeting, External Thinkers can come up with their best ideas, or thought processes, and turn right around and crystallize their ideas and concepts.

The drawback is that External Thinkers many times are verbalizing and not listening to others. There isn't much verbalizing taking place when you are listening, is there?

How External Thinkers operate

External Thinkers are more innately heads up. They are aware and they look at their environment more. That is because they are looking for feedback, especially positive feedback from the people who are valuable to them. They want answers, and if you are valued and can help, then your input is highly important to them.

Sometimes, External Thinkers will keep on verbalizing until they get a response.

Is there such thing as introverted External Thinker? Not really, but if you think you may be introverted and an external thinker at the same time, then talking to a lot of people would be draining — but being stuck in an office and not talking to people would be even more draining. If that describes you, then you are probably as close to being an introverted External Thinker as is possible.

External thinkers are usually great at reading people and use that skill to get the response they want from others!

Typically, External Thinkers are extroverts, but that doesn't mean they are necessarily outgoing and gregarious. These two aspects of our nature, being outgoing and gregarious, can be highly affected by our upbringing.

What is challenging with External Thinkers is that they can send mixed signals. It's as if they are part chameleon. They can modify their persona to get the response necessary from the people who are important to them. Does that send mixed signals? Sure it does! The External Thinker operates according to this mantra:

"I want a response and will modify my verbalization to get the response I need."

As a result, they will modify themselves based upon getting a response from the parties important to them.

Prior to me discovering how people are hard wired, my wife and I were driving to a party and we got into an argument in the car.

As an External Thinker I used my verbal skills to get responses from her. In all honesty, I did pull out a few good verbal barbs as our argument got quite heated and she had ticked me off. We pulled into the driveway of the home hosting the party. I jumped out of the car — all smiles — and went to meet everyone. My wife could not believe it! We had been arguing moments before and then I'm all smiles! It took her a few minutes to adjust herself (the Internal Thinker) and then she came to meet everyone.

Have you ever been called a "chameleon"?

Driving home she asked me: "How could you be nasty with me one minute and pleasant with everyone else the next?"

I responded: "Well, you made me mad in the argument, so my responses to you weren't so pleasant — the people at the party hadn't done anything, why should I be unpleasant with them?"

Ahh, the perspective that the External Thinker may at times be seen as the chameleon!

So what happens when two External Thinkers deal with each other? They play off each other, as both need to verbalize their thoughts out loud, and will modify ideas and thoughts as they verbalize. Two External Thinkers can sit down to discuss one topic and then — seven different issues later — come up with a resolution to the topic they initially decided to discuss.

Since External Thinkers like response and validation of their ideas, they also like personal recognition for those thoughts and ideas. "What a great thought — you rock!" really makes the External Thinker smile!

Again, the more you know the more effective you can be in your relationships!

CHAPTER #9

Something's Happening Behind That Blank Stare!

If you find yourself going into your own head when someone verbalizes and wants a response — otherwise known as the giver of the blank stare — there is a reason for it! Internal Thinkers will talk to people for information, but do not initially respond until they have had time to think the idea, concept or point of discussion through. If that's you, then it makes great sense.

Does this sound like you as well: you want some degree of people interaction, but a lot of face-to-face verbal communication is just downright draining! You need some element of quiet time to process and think through all of the verbalization you receive from others.

Understanding the Internal Thinker

Internal Thinkers will listen to what everybody says. Then they will take time to think about what they've heard. During that time of regurgitating and thinking is when they generate their best ideas and responses.

My wife likes to think things through before reaching a conclusion. In fact, she does NOT want to respond until she has had time to process. In addition, she does NOT want to be verbally forced to provide a response until she has had adequate time to think and process.

If I keep talking and talking, the more it impedes her from processing and understanding. Her mantra, just as it is with every Internal Thinker, is: "What you see is what you get." You get the blank stare until the Internal Thinker has had time to internally crystallize; you get direct responses when the Internal Thinker responds; and you **Internal Thinkers** don't get the chameleon as Internal Thinkers **are innately heads** are more direct in the communication process **down.** and do not need to modify their approach with people to get a response.

Interestingly, it isn't only the External Thinkers that can struggle with effective listening. Internal Thinkers can struggle with listening because they block everything out as they think and process. This is one of the reasons my wife would go away to Pluto when I over verbalized. She would start thinking about something I said and during her thought process, did not listen to the rest of what I was saying.

Internal Thinkers are innately heads down. They don't like a lot of verbal expression and excess verbiage is just a load of words that create a lot of clutter. Give them time to walk away from the clutter and their thoughts will become clearer.

It is important to recognize that Internal Thinkers hate being blind-sided by something they haven't prepared their thoughts for, but it is their very nature to require time to create an appropriate response. They need to be patient with those who come up with a new verbal topic that they have not had time to internally digest, which is typically the External Thinker. And External Thinkers need to give Internal Thinkers room and time to respond. An easy approach — just ask them when they can get back with you on a decision!

Internal Thinkers often become frustrated with themselves when they cannot come up with an immediate answer right away. I'm not saying "What do you want for lunch?" but decisions that do require a bit of contemplation. Internal Thinkers will look at External thinkers and wonder why they are not as adept at developing a resolution to an issue as quickly and as verbally as an External Thinker.

Just knowing your wiring — your specific channel — can bring inner satisfaction as well as better understanding of those around you.

How does this help me?

Once you understand your wiring — your specific channel — if you are an Internal Thinker or an External Thinker, you will see what motivates you from a communication standpoint. That is because communication is not just about talking.

We all talk, but some of us are more verbal thinkers/talkers and some of us are internal thinkers/talkers. Do you get energized when you've had the opportunity to verbalize? Do you get drained from too much face-to-face verbal interaction? Do you get great ideas during a meeting? Or do you get great ideas a few hours later after you have had a chance to think?

Our natural energy comes from our innate hardwiring. When we respond to situations from our natural channels, we get energized from being able to process in that manner. External Thinkers get energized by verbalizing; Internal Thinkers get energized with alone time to think issues through!

The more you understand yourself and those around you, the more effectively you will communicate and function in your areas of influence. You won't take things as personally as you did before and will realize it is just a function of the person's channels.

You'll be a better listener, and you'll be more aware of those around you. When you learn your specific hardwiring and your specific channels — as well as the specific channels of those around you — you will be able to interact better with people. The result is that you are a better leader, follower, spouse, or friend.

Develop and use the common language

Let people know who you are and encourage them to know you! If you are an External Thinker let others know: "I'm an External Thinker and do best when I can verbalize my thoughts." If you are an Internal Thinker let others know: "I'm an Internal Think and will respond after I have had time to think about what you've said."

The above is so easy and will solve many of the communication issues you face with others!

Key Points to Remember:

1) *External Thinkers interacting with External Thinkers*

When two or more External Thinkers interact, keep the following in mind:

· Let each person finish their statements and give time for the other to verbalize.
· Since External Thinkers crystallize thoughts when they verbalize, many times External Thinkers will jump in on a conversation to express themselves.

2) *External Thinkers interacting with Internal Thinkers*

· External Thinkers: Allow the Internal Thinker time to think. If you see the blank stare, just ask: "Do you need time to think about this before responding?"
· Internal Thinkers: Create several different responses when dealing with External Thinkers. "Let me noodle

on this." "You make some good points, let me digest them." "Can I get back to you on this later?"

· Internal Thinkers please note. If you say you are going to get back with the External Thinker, get back with them! Make communication an agenda item (write it down to get back with them) as Internal Thinkers do have the tendency to think about their answer, have the conversation in their head and then not get back to the other individual!

3) Internal Thinkers interacting with Internal Thinkers

· The biggest issue with Internal Thinkers dealing with each other is that both want to think before responding. Sometimes both will think about an issue, resolve it internally and not communicate to the other. For example, many IT departments in companies are filled with Internal Thinkers. They like the heads down environment of IT. Two technicians may work right next to each other, chat during the day, but not communicate the really important items.

The simple solution is to make communication an agenda item. Write down the specific item you are considering, the person who the response is intended and the time deadline for a response. Once the Internal Thinker has relayed their thoughts, the item can be crossed off the list and effective communication lives!

Your goal is always to interact better with people.

SECTION IV:

HIGH / LOW PRESSURE OPERATOR CHANNEL

CHAPTER #10

I'm Laid Back — You're Wound Up!

My mom used to have drawers underneath her bed in which she stored things. Normal enough … but she had an instruction sheet that showed what was neatly stashed in every single drawer around the bed! It was like a detailed storage map.

What was that all about? Was it really necessary?

It was her way of creating her own order and following her own plan, and to her, it was necessary. We all do it to our own degree of desired peace and calm. We want to control, or not control, the element of predictability.

Hidden within this element of predictability is an incredibly important factor that applies to us all. It is the speed of decision making.

Take my mom, for example. She could whip out her little map and tell you in less than 15 seconds exactly what she had stored under her bed, and then pull it out in another 15 seconds.

Those who think it's borderline psychotic to have a storage map for a bed are the ones who will be rooting and rummaging around, trying to find what they think they put in there. If they find it at all, I would bet you that they wouldn't have it out in less than 30 seconds!

Everything in sequence

How fast can you make a decision? That's really a complicated question because decision making involves so many pieces, such as gathering all the information, knowing the options, being aware of schedules, doing what's right, and so on.

If you were to break it all down into little pieces, it would be a matter of sequence. One detail follows upon the next, and the next, and so on. How fast these items are lined up in sequence, either on paper or in your mind, is how fast you can make your decisions.

How fast can you make a decision? In your own world, be it your home or workplace, you are faced with countless variables and options. The degree that you order your environment and arrange things in sequence is entirely up to you, but it speaks volumes about how you like to operate.

Do you demand as much, or more, predictability than my mother? Or do you prefer a looser, freer, less detailed approach? There is, as you know, no wrong answer, but your answer is your unique style.

Why is order so important?

Order is important for what it offers you, like neat straight lines on a piece of paper. You know where things are, you know what to do, and there are no surprises. It's predictable.

But the varying need or demand for order is really a door to something even bigger, something even more complex. This powerful quality is the element of pressure.

How much pressure can you take and still function at your peak performance level? My mother, as you can imagine, did not like pressure. She naturally did her best to minimize pressure, thus the lists, maps, order, and sequence.

But there are others who absolutely thrive on pressure. The more balls in the air, the more objects in motion, the happier they are. They eat it up and want more!

What about you? Do you thrive on pressure, does it push you to run faster and do more? Or does pressure shut you down and make you wish you hadn't gotten out of bed?

In truth, we are all somewhere on the scale between Low-Pressure operators and High-Pressure operators.

When low-pressure and high-pressure collide

I feel like a weatherman, talking about low-pressure and high-pressure systems, but when you see these two operators collide, you'll think you stepped into a twister! I've seen these collisions, and you have as well. They can be dangerous.

Let's take the common occurrence of interruptions. We have them at home, at work, on the road, just about anywhere, and we all need to learn how to accept interruptions. It's a part of life that is unavoidable. However, as I know some of you are thinking, just because you have to accept them doesn't mean you have to like them!

I agree, you don't have to like interruptions (not many people do), but some people accept the interruption while with others the interruption distracts them from what they are focused on.

For Low-Pressure operators, they want most things they do presented in an orderly basis. From information to following a plan to making a decision. Why? Because of their wiring, they prefer to attack things in a sequential manner — completing one before moving onto two. If you happen to interrupt Low-Pressure operators in the middle of a process, they'll simply start over. It's their gifting.

And when you talk with Low-Pressure operators, they will stop what they are doing and give you their full attention. They want to complete their conversation with you (start and stop) and then move on.

Some thrive, and some dive, when they are under pressure.

High-Pressure operators, on the other hand, are just the opposite! They will listen to you ... as they watch the clock, check emails (if you are on the phone with them), wave at co-workers, send a text message, or even make an order online. Focusing in on a conversation is agreeably the wise and considerate thing to do, but it may feel like an impossible task at times.

And as for interruptions, the more the merrier! High-Pressure operators thrive on more balls in the air. If one task splits into two, and then into four, they are on it. No problem.

You could say that Low-Pressure operators are a very mild decaf coffee, while high-pressure operators are pure black, liquid caffeine. In its place, both are of value.

Which are you?

CHAPTER #11

You've Got Me Under the Gun, But I Love the Pressure!

We all face pressures in life, but the key difference is that some of us purposefully put more pressure on ourselves and on others to perform. That's right; some of us actually turn UP the pressure volume on purpose! The High-Pressure operators crank it up because it makes everything work, flow and groove better.

For the Low-Pressure operators, they seek to minimize the pressure. "Turn it down!" their minds are screaming, and they do all they can to ratchet down the pressures that are building around them.

High-Pressure operators are also known as "jugglers." They somehow balance countless tasks and duties, all while picking up even more things to do. Of course, you might be thinking, there is a point of critical mass where it all comes crashing down, but jugglers will flirt with such disaster, time and time again.

The end result is that you, or your employees or just people you know who are High-Pressure operators, will get a lot accomplished in a short period of time. The drawback will be that sometimes you'll have to pick up the pieces from spinning plates that fall to the ground. This might be projects dropped, schedules missed, or plans changed at the last minute. The less the better, naturally, but it's a factor that must be considered.

High-Pressure operators thrive when they have multiple items on their things to do list. Only one item on the list and it is hard to get motivated. Twenty things on the list and they are ready to go.

What High-Pressure operators thrive on

High-pressure operators focus on immediate needs, doing what needs to be done now, so the prospect of doing the same things day in and day out will drive them bonkers. Repetition is boredom, but jumping from item to item is much more exciting and it allows for variety.

This same jumping from one thing to the next influences High-Pressure operators to make quick decisions. Focusing for too long on one item is, after all, boring and painful.

Pressure will energize or de-energize you. Which is it?

Be aware, whether this applies to you or not, that High-Pressure operators want others to jump from task to task, make quick decisions, and enjoy the same elements of pressure. This is certainly not realistic, but it is an innate desire nonetheless. Why? It's the channel that energizes them, so everyone should be energized by this chaos.

High-Pressure operators like to interrupt when they have something to say because they can't stand the wait. In fact, they want to cut to the end of an informational conversation. "Get on with it," they are thinking. Naturally, they have a hard time understanding Low-Pressure operators who will actually wait their turn to speak because they enjoy a sense of sequence from their channeled environment.

Do you have a hard time sitting all day long? Do you need to be be-bopping around? Maybe you wondered if you had an invisible spring in your chair. If so, you are probably a High-Pressure operator.

Aren't sure if that defines you? Here's the final clue. Do you turn everything into a high-pressure situation? High-Pressure operators know that if they want to get something done that they must actually create pressure to motivate themselves. This makes good sense to high-pressure operators, creating what they need for their own environment even if it is more pressure, and if you do it, then it sounds like you are a high-pressure operator.

As with every channel, the strength of High-Pressure operators is the ability to juggle multiple tasks; the limitation is that sometimes things do fall through the cracks!

CHAPTER #12

Let Me Finish One Thing Before I Start the Next

    We buy frozen foods from a home service delivery company. Our delivery guy is a great example of a Low-Pressure operator (which makes him perfect for route sales). He's at our door every other Tuesday at 6:10 p.m. and he says the same thing to my wife, "What would you like today?"

    She gives him the list, he gets the items from the back of the truck, and he brings them to her and says, "Thank you very much." He then walks out, looks back, and says, "I'll see you in two weeks."

What is interesting is the fact that he delivered to my neighbor's door for three years and never once bothered to walk over to our house to see if we were interested in getting the same home delivery. My wife actually started getting the products delivered at her work, but it was a challenge keeping the items frozen during the work day and then bringing all the stuff home.

So, one Tuesday evening when I saw the truck pull up at our neighbor's house, I walked over and said, "Hey, would you mind stopping at our house?"

He replied, "Well, I can stop by later after I've finished my other stops. We can then put you on the route for every other Tuesday."

In my opinion, it appeared as though there was no motivation for the sale! There was, but his primary goal was to finish what he had started before he picked up anything else. The new sale would come after he had finished his route.

And then we would receive regular service.

There is no pressure to be anything that you are not.

He did come back for the order later that night and has provided us great service ever since. As a High-Pressure operator, I expected him to drop everything for the order. As a Low-Pressure operator he wanted to finish with his current route — after all taking care of me would have disrupted the plan and he would then be late for his other stops. He did take care of me, just after he finished with his current route.

For the Low-Pressure Operator, finishing the established plan, then taking on new tasks not only fits their wiring, but is the most efficient way to operate!

Understanding Low-Pressure operators

Low-Pressure operators are Low-Pressure operators because that is the channel that is part of their wiring. They don't like any added pressure. When High-Pressure operators come around and start cranking up the pressure to get things done now, it drives Low-Pressure operators crazy!

They don't need the added pressure because they have an innate ability to focus on work or decisions and keep going until the job is done. They are driven within to complete one task before moving onto the next.

How do you increase accomplishment for low-pressure operators? You give them time to finish a project. It doesn't necessarily mean that if they are involved in a two month project that nothing can occur during that time interval. It just means Low-Pressure operators function best when given time to finish or button down one thing before moving onto the next.

The same is true for decision making. Give them time to deliberate on issues before they make their decision.

Does that sound like you?

Interestingly, Low-Pressure operators perform worse in all situations, whether it's a task or a decision, if they are faced with a lot of pressure. And no doubt, it's all "unnecessary" pressure! What's more, Low-Pressure operators actually get their self-confidence from a sense of order — having a plan and following it step by step until completion. The plan may be performing a task or the plan may be deliberating a decision.

If you wonder if you are a Low-Pressure operator, then consider the answer to these questions:

· Do you want order in your environment?
· Do you wait patiently in conversations for the sake of order?
· Are you more deliberate and thorough in your decision making?
· Do you try consciously to minimize pressure?
· Do you enjoy total focus on a project or from others when having a conversation?

We need Low-Pressure operators just as badly as we need High-Pressure operators, so there is no pressure (no pun intended) to be anything that you are not.

You'll often find Low-Pressure operators in an accounting, software development, or a health care job where things are systematically driven. A heart surgeon, for example, is extremely sequentially driven. There's a step, a process, and an order to every surgery ... for you don't want them missing any steps if you are the one going under the knife!

Are you a Low-Pressure operator or a High-Pressure operator? I think you know. If you're still not sure, the self assessment in Chapter 18 should provide the answer!

Develop and use the common language

Let people know who you are and encourage them to know you.

I bet you know which you are: a Low-Pressure or High-Pressure operator.

If you are Low Pressure, let others know: "I'm a Low-Pressure Operator and do best when you do not pressure the decision." OR "I'm a Low-Pressure operator and need time to deliberate on the decision. I will get back with you when I said I would."

If you are High Pressure let others know: "I'm a High-Pressure operator, relay things to me quick and I'll make a fast decision." OR "I'm a High-Pressure operator so I do best with many things on my plate!"

Using common language statements keeps a person's channels "real" to others. While the perception is that High-Pressure operators drink too much caffeine and Low-Pressure operators don't drink enough of those caffeinated products, the perception is based upon the individual channel of how each person is wired. Eliminating the mystery of people lends to better understanding and actually creates faster decisions and fewer frustrations!

Key Points to Remember:

1) High-Pressure operators interacting with High-Pressure operators

- Each understand that the tendency is to pile too many activities on their plates. Eliminate some of those to the truly important issues.
- Since both want to make quick decisions, make the decision, but then review to ensure it wasn't made too quick.
- Limit interrupting each other!

2) High-Pressure operators interacting with Low-Pressure operators

- High-Pressure operators: Take a deep breath and calm yourself down (the Low-Pressure operator will appreciate the lack of visible caffeine).
- High-Pressure operators: Give Low-Pressure operators time to button one thing down before focusing on the next. It can be as simple as: "I need you to switch gears. How long until you can button down what you are working on?"
- High-Pressure operators: Focus on the Low-Pressure operator when conversing. Remember that doing 17 things at the same time when they are having a conversation is very distracting to the Low-Pressure operator. Actually, when you focus only on them, the conversation goes quicker!
- High-Pressure operators: When the Low-Pressure operator tells you when they'll have a decision, they will have the decision then! Additional pressure to speed up the decision only slows it down.
- Low-Pressure operators: Expect interruptions and the demand for a quick decision. My guess is that if you are a Low-Pressure operator you have grown to expect this.

Use the common language and let them know how to best interact with you!

· Note: There are many hints above for the High-Pressure operators, but only one for the Low-Pressure operator. The reason is that historically High-Pressure operators due to their impatience — are the ones to create interruptions, want quick decisions and don't let others finish one before moving onto two!

3) Low-Pressure operators interacting with Low-Pressure operators

· Since both are patient, calm deliberate decision makers who operate best sequentially, they will naturally interact well. The biggest issue is getting decisions made on an agreed upon time table. After all, what one Low-Pressure operator feels is time to deliberate a decision (48 hours) may not be what the other Low-Pressure operator needs to make the same decision (72 hours). Discuss what each of you had in mind for a time table and agree to something that meets both Low-Pressure operator needs!

SECTION V:

BULLET POINT / PROOFER INFORMATION CHANNEL

CHAPTER #13

What's Your Point?

A husband and wife were about to buy a new refrigerator. The wife wanted to gather all the data, such as storage capacity, warranty, dimensions, and explanation of all the features, everything necessary to make a solid decision on the refrigerator.

Before leaving home, the husband and wife agreed that they would do their homework before buying. Then they went to town.

As they entered the appliance store, the husband asked the nearest salesperson, "Which one makes ice?" The sales rep pointed to the closest refrigerator and the husband responded, "Sold!"

Sound familiar?
If the shoe fits, wear it!

The above story is funny, but it's also very true. You either have tendencies like the husband (a "Bullet Pointer") or like the wife (a "Proofer"), but there are no other options. So which is it? Let me help you.

You are a Bullet Pointer if:

· You want only the basic critical points of information (if you want more, you'll ask for it; but want only the basics first).
· You are actually bothered by a lot of information.
· You are less cautious in the decision making process.
· You do not want or require high elements of proven information.
· You ignore the proof and follow what you want to do.
· You tune out with too much information.

On the other hand, you are a Proofer if:

· You want significant facts and figures in making decisions.
· You like information because it reduces your chances of making a mistake in the decision making process.
· You are cautious and want some degree of "proven" information.
· You are frustrated when you don't receive enough information.
· You enjoy elements of structure in your world.
· You want and give high degrees of information.

Hopefully you know which you are, a Proofer or a Bullet Pointer. We all need and enjoy elements of information within our environment. How we are wired determines just how much information we require.

It's important to note that neither the husband nor the wife were wrong about their approach to buying a refrigerator. I would suggest, however, for the sake of fiscal responsibility, wise purchasing, and marital harmony that the Proofer (the wife, in this case) be the one who makes the final call on purchases over a certain price.

There is no shame in asking for help. I think it's a sign of wisdom to ask for help because it shows that you know how you think and operate (your channel) … and it shows that you are aware of the wiring and skill sets in other people. You are observant and proactive, which are ingredients for success.

Why is information so important?

The amount of information people seek correlates exactly with the amount of risk they accept in the decision-making process. This correlation has nothing to do with education, intellect, or the type of risk involved. Rather, it's just how we make decisions.

I'm the type of person who can make a decision with very little information and still sleep at night. It's all about risk, and I'm extremely comfortable dealing with it, for if I'm proved wrong, so be it.

My wife, on the other hand, will always require reams of proof before making any type of decision important to her. She's not from the "show me" state of Missouri, but her wiring requires that she be shown proof. No proof, no buy-in, no decision!

The information you require is proportional to your level of risk taking in decision making.

Being on the opposite ends of the risk scale has helped us balance our lives accordingly. I wish she had been present in my life many years ago, as she would have helped stop me from making some very bad decisions. She, in turn, has said that my acceptance of risk would have helped her not agonize so long and seek exhaustive amounts of evidence to support whatever she wanted to do. Clearly, our hard wiring is what determines how much evidence we need to make decisions and to minimize the possibility of failure.

When it comes to information, are you a Proofer or a Bullet Pointer?

91

CHAPTER #14

The Summary Sheet, Please!

The innate hardwiring of Bullet Pointers not wanting a lot of proven information correlates to them not wanting much structure in their channeled environment. In addition, they look at the established rules and regulations as the "exception handbook" — if there is a rule, there must be an accompanying exception.

This does not mean that Bullet Pointers are amoral or break the laws, they just don't need all the facts and figures and proven information in the decision making process. Too much information just makes them tune out. Bullet Pointers are the ones who say, "It's easier to ask for forgiveness than it is to ask for permission."

Out in the real world

The willingness to accept risk or minimize the chance of failure in decision-making is certainly apparent in the business world. My research in this area has focused on the strife that inevitably exists between the sales and operations areas of most companies. Working with various organizations, I have noted a common pattern in the way sales people (typically Bullet Pointers) and operations personnel (typically Proofers) make decisions and accept risk.

As you can imagine, these two butt heads regularly!

While conducting a training session at a food-processing firm, I saw this very issue come to light. Company policy dictated that developing quotes for new customers required a two-week time period. The reason was that the operations department had to actually create the food product to determine the exact amount of each ingredient, develop the packaging, determine the volume to be produced, and ultimately determine the exact costs, thus the selling price.

> Out in the real world, people seem to do strange things ... wouldn't it be great to understand why?

That's a lot of required work for the operations department to get done in the two-week period ... but consistently this company's sales manager would call on a prospect, return to the office, and inform the operations department that he needed a full quote in three days! This, of course, frustrated the operations manager and created "unnecessary" havoc, stress, pressure, and work.

I met with the managers of both departments to see if we could come up with a workable solution. The operations manager (a Proofer who needed a considerable amount of information to eliminate risk in his decision-making) was providing the sales manager (a Bullet Pointer who only needed bullet points and was comfortable dealing with ballpark estimates) with two weeks of reports, data, answers, and information.

Do you see the solution here?

First, I got each manager to comprehend the comfort level of risk that the other required. Second, since details were not particularly important to the Bullet Pointer sales manager, the operations manager agreed to provide an abbreviated report. And third, the sales manager understood and agreed not to force the Proofer operations manager to get results in three short days.

In essence, they tuned into each other and agreed to work around each other's needs accordingly. The end result was better inner-office workings and better reports for prospective customers.

It became a win-win relationship, which is the goal of understanding Proofers and Bullet Pointers.

CHAPTER #15

Give Me Serious Proof!

One night, a Proofer set his alarm clock and went to bed. Next door, at the same moment, a Bullet Pointer was setting his alarm clock.

The next morning, both happened to be in line at a coffee shop on their way to work.

"How are you this fine day?" asked the lady behind the counter.

The Proofer replied,

"Well, okay, but I'm running a bit behind today. I set my alarm last night, but at 5:28 it went off. Strange thing, since I always set it for 5:30. Well, I hit the snooze alarm to grab 10 more minutes of sleep. The alarm went off at 5:39 instead of 5:38. I hit the snooze button again, and this time the alarm went off at 5:42 instead of 5:48. Something must be wrong with my clock. So when I finally arose I spent the next 15 minutes trying to figure out what was wrong with the clock. That's what made me late. But here I am."

After he stepped aside with his coffee, the lady asked the Bullet Pointer, "How are you this fine day?"

The Bullet Pointer, who amazingly had the exact same thing happen with his alarm clock, responded,

"A little delayed this morning, but otherwise doing well."

Both believed they had relayed the same amount of detail. The Proofer gave all the details and facts. Why? Because Proofers want all the details and facts! The Bullet Pointer gave only the basic summary points.

Why? Because Bullet Pointers only want the summary points!

Giving Proofers what they need

As we've discussed, Proofers like proof and details. They like elements of structure and they need rules enforced. The structure creates an adherence to rules and regulations, which is just more proven information on how to make decisions and operate within the work or home environment.

Proofers give ALL the facts and details because they need the facts and details!

As you can imagine, sometimes Proofers can never get enough information. Place a Proofer in an environment of loose schedules and much flexibility and the Proofer will ask, "How can anything be enforced?" They aren't asking if anything can be accomplished, but if things can be controlled. Why? Because Proofers get their self-confidence externally from the amount of proof, data, and information they have.

So, if you want to give Proofers what they need, then give them clear and unambiguous information with lots of details. Throw in some feedback, maybe through some analytical data, and the Proofers will be operating at peak levels. They need consistency through equitable and fair distribution of rules and regulations within a defined structure.

As a Proofer or Bullet Pointer, what do you do?

Proofers need a lot of information, Bullet Pointers need less, and this often creates roadblocks between people who are striving to make decisions for themselves.

Haven't you faced challenges in this area? Not getting enough information? Or getting too much? Either way, it's a challenge to get what you actually need. (By inference, I'm also saying that it's a challenge to give what others actually need, but that can be dealt with when you understand yourself and the other person.)

Bullet Pointers give ONLY the basic summary points.

The solution is pretty straightforward: Recognize why people facing the same decision may each demand a different amount of information. The reason "why" relates directly to the fact that some of us are Proofers and some of us are Bullet Pointers.

Based on what you now know, think about the Bullet Pointer husband who bought the refrigerator based on the fact that it made ice. That was a pretty silly thing to do, primarily because he completely tossed out all the information that his Proofer wife had gathered, information that would have been helpful in making a wise decision.

But wouldn't it have been a gut-wrenching, mind-numbing experience if you had demanded that he gather all the necessary data that his wife demanded? That would have totally frustrated him, and you probably would never get the information you requested.

In addition, what if you asked the Proofer wife to make a quick decision without sufficient information? That would instantly drive her stress levels through the roof, making further discussion impossible. It is literally scary and completely against the grain for Proofers to make decisions with little or no information.

Whether you are looking to improve your marriage, relationships, or work environment, it pays to understand how Proofers and Bullet Pointers think and operate. Your job is then to figure out who is who (Chapter 18) and put that knowledge to good use!

Develop and use the common language

Let people know who you are and encourage them to know you!

If you are a Bullet Pointer, let others know: "I'm a Bullet Point person, please just give me the basic points." OR "As a Bullet Pointer, just the summary sheet of information please."

If you are a Proofer, let others know: "I'm a Proofer and like lots of detail and solid data in decision making." OR "As a Proofer I like serious proof — please provide me detail and all of the whys."

You absolutely must tell others how you operate. You must!

Using common language statements keeps a person's channels "real" to others. While the perception is that Bullet Pointers make quick decisions regardless of fact and Proofers suffer from too much analysis, the perception is based upon the channel of the person's wiring. Eliminating the mystery of people lends to better understanding and actually creates better interactions and less frustrations!

Key Points to Remember:

1) Bullet Pointers interacting with Bullet Pointers

· Make sure that your summary sheet of information matches their summary sheet of information. Two Bullet Pointers may not always be on the same page.

· Ask for clarification of points if the summary sheet is too vague.

2) *Bullet Pointers interacting with Proofers*

· Bullet Pointers: Use illustrative examples to make sure enough data has been relayed. For example, a Bullet Pointer may look at a Proofer and say "write me a report on our competitors," which will create a dazed look from the Proofer as they are filled with questions for more data. Instead, "write me a report on our competi- tors like you did for me last year, the one page summary on our three primary market rivals."
· Proofers: Start out giving the Bullet Pointer the summary sheet of data instead of all of the details. Keep in mind that if the Bullet Pointer wants more data, they'll ask for it!

3) *Proofers interacting with Proofers*

· Since both are driven for data and proof, each will prob- ably provide the other with enough information and data.
· Be aware that too much data and information can create "analysis paralysis" between the two and no decision gets made!

101

SECTION VI:

MAKING SENSE OF IT ALL

CHAPTER #16

Putting It All Together

We've thrown a lot of words around in this book, like "hardwiring" and "channel," not to mention all the terms that describe those things called people. The goal has never been to confuse you. Rather, life is confusing enough as it is! The terms help us put a "handle" on something so that we can both name it and hold on at the same time.

Remember, your "hardwiring" is how you are put together as a person and your "channel" is the side you fall on from each of the four main factors discussed.

For example, your "hardwiring" may be Dominator, External Thinker, Low Pressure Operator and Bullet Pointer. The "channel" is the specific layer we are discussing. In this case the four channels are the Dominator (for ideas and environmental control); External Thinker as how you verbalize to crystallize thought; Low Pressure operator (sequentially driven and likes order) and Bullet Pointer (just the summary sheet.)

We need to consider all four "channels" when looking at how someone is "hardwired." Why? It explains the whole person.

An Internal Thinker who is also a Proofer wants time to think about and digest information. And understanding how you react is integral to your success!

Understanding how you react is integral to your success!

External Thinker who is also a Proofer wants time to verbalize the information. See the difference?

In re-cap, at the core, we have worked to understand how we and other people react to Dominance, Communication, Pressure, and Decision Making. All the other terms come into play, based on these four simple words that turn out to be so very complex!

Understanding how you work, and how others work, will indeed make all the difference in the world.

Now that you get the wiring channels ...

Now you understand those who have never had kids, yet they are more than willing to tell you all the things you are doing wrong with your own children. This also describes the person who isn't married but has plenty of marriage advice. They need no information to validate their opinion, and they are fine with that.

Now you understand why some of us, when told not to touch the hot stove, we had to go touch the hot stove! We simply had to prove it to ourselves. Does this understanding not help us with our kids, our spouse, and others? Understanding people better helps you remove the clouds of ambiguity around them. We all see the world differently, and interestingly, nobody is wrong. It is just a different perspective.

No wonder we are so different! And no wonder we feel that some people are downright rude and insensitive.

Now you understand what makes people go crazy. One of my clients runs his own computer business, and on the side, he and his wife run a marriage enhancement program at their church. He asked me to come in and do a presentation. There were 20 couples and we talked about the same things you've read in this book. There was one couple in the meeting that had been married for 12 years ... and they had been in marriage counseling for 11 years! They both liked their way of doing things best and they would draw a line in the sand and dare each other to cross it because challenge and head butting was a good thing. Their tendency was to keep information tight to the chest and not communicate which each other very well. They were very rigid with things and neither one of them wanted to lose, so they weren't ever going to file for divorce because that was a loss.

At the break, I was headed to the restroom when they grabbed me and pulled me aside. They said, "Thank you! We finally know why we do what we do." The counselors had told them to "talk about it," but more talking wasn't the issue. They simply didn't understand who they were on the inside, and who the other person was. Once they figured that out, the actions made sense. And — most importantly — a positive solution was created. This couple is still together today, but instead of attending non-stop marriage improvement classes, they are enjoying their time together!

Will you improve with age?

Yes, like wine, you will get better with age ... but your internal hardwiring and ways of doing things will not change all that much over time. I've actually tested the same people twice, with many years of living life in between, and the results show that the person is still the same person. Yes, some rough edges may have been smoothed down, some of the communication skills improved out of necessity, but for the most part, nothing has changed.

What that means is that you can improve and modify yourself, but you cannot be someone else. You should take that as a compliment. The truth is you don't want to be a duplicate of someone else. Honestly, if there are two of you, then one of you isn't needed!

Your family, friends, co-workers and employer need you, the unique you.

Are there benefits to figuring people out?

There are countless benefits to figuring people out, and that includes you figuring you out!

Stress comes when you try to be who you are not. You were wired the way you were wired. End of story. Sure, you'll feel stress in life, whether it's work or home related, but when you know who you are on the inside and you know how and why you operate the way you do, the stress will be much more manageable.

We are who we are, and we are wired the way we are wired.

You will be less confused by the actions of others when you understand why they do what they do. It will make sense. "Now I know why the boss never does that" or "Now I understand why the teacher says that."

Whatever the example, whoever the person, the "Oh, I get it" response will put your mind and heart at ease.

And if you are an employer, you will never need to, only 90 days after hiring someone, say to yourself, "Who is this person I hired?" Some people, by their very nature, interview extremely well but perform poorly. Some people may not interview very well but might be better suited for the job. You can now go past what prospective hires say and look at what actually makes them tick.

Whatever your situation, the more you understand about those around you, the better off you will be.

Take the questionnaire in Chapter 18 — do one on you and one on another you know well. Let it be the beginning of a beautiful future ... a future that is clear, focused, understandable, and fulfilling!

CHAPTER #17

So What?!

Let's put this all together with one final real life story that takes into account my hardwiring, my wife's hardwiring and our individual channels.

A few years ago, Jeannie and I decided that it was time to do some remodeling around our house and that it would be a great (?) experience to do all of the work ourselves. After all, doing it ourselves would be fun. Talk about a massive DIY project! We did all the work, and neither my wife nor I are real "construction oriented" people.

I called my stepson, who is in construction, and I asked him how long he thought it would take me to do one of the projects, including caulking the room. He said, "Jay, one hour." Of course, 8 hours and 10 tubes of caulk later, I was still working on it. Just a bit of flavor on how much fun the DIY project was becoming.

We had to have the house done by November 18th of that year because we were having window treatments installed in the whole house on the 19th, and all carpeting and floors done on the

20th because we had company arriving on the 22nd for a family wedding on the 30th.

We started in January we knew we had about 10 months to do all the work. Plenty of time, even for beginner DIY people! It was a great plan, but we didn't follow it very well. By September, we were horribly behind. We both decided we were going to take a week off of work and with the two weekends, have 9 straight days in order to get caught up.

Right about then my wife's son, who lives in Baltimore, called us. "Hey," he said innocently, "instead of you guys working so hard on the house, why don't you come on out to Baltimore and visit with us for a couple days."

My wife turned to me, "My son needs me to come visit him. I know we have 9 days set aside to work, but we're not going to do that. Instead, we are going to take 4 of them and go to Baltimore."

I quickly replied, "There's no way we're going to Baltimore. I can't believe you agreed to go because we have a lot of work to get done. It just doesn't make any sense! In my mind we are not going to go to Baltimore."

Her answer was short and sweet, "We're going to Baltimore."

At that point, I thought to myself, "You know, Jay, you handled it all wrong."

STOP!

What happened?

I came at Jeannie from my hardwiring, my particular channels.

- Dominator: I told her what was going to happen.
- External Thinker: I was very verbal and expected to just talk the issue out.
- High Pressure: I responded quickly.
- Bullet Pointer: I did not provide any facts or data to support my position.

So the next morning while we were having coffee, I decided to have the same conversation, but appeal to Jeannie's particular channels in her hardwiring and said, "Honey, do you want the house done when the company arrives on the 22nd of November or isn't it important to you?"

She replied, "Oh no, no, no, no, I want the house done."

I said, "Well, you know, it is always wonderful to see Craig & Melanie in Baltimore, but they are going to be spending 8 days with us at the end of November and since you want the house done by the 22nd, we can get the guest room done, the den done because the in-laws will be coming over for a little party, and we can finish up the office, which were all the things that you wanted to get done. But you know what; I can't talk about this right now. I have an appointment, so we'll talk about it when I get home." I gave her the reasons that not going to Baltimore and working on the house would achieve the results she wanted — her way. When I got home that night, she said, "I've decided we're not going to Baltimore."

It was that simple!

WHY?

Quite simply, Jeannie is best interacted with when using her channels:

- · Dominator: She has to have her input and thumbprint on the idea or plan of action.
- · Internal Thinker: She needed time to think internally about our conversation to provide her clearest thoughts.
- · High Pressure: She responded the first time very quickly the evening before (remember her "no") and did respond quickly the second time around, but after time to think.
- · Proofer: Jeannie needed details to better formulate her decision.

You see, with any Dominator it is important that you present ideas that will help them get their results. Let them put their thumbprint on the ideas to gain acceptance. When I first confronted Jeannie, it was all about my results, my way. When we spoke the next morning, it was about her getting her results, her way. As I said earlier, Dominators may appear, but are not obstinate about things — they just thrive when the idea becomes their idea — complete with their input!

Prior to understanding hard wiring, the initial conversation (and many ensuing conversations about going to Baltimore or finishing the house) would have resulted in arguing and fighting. Since we were able to discuss without the arguments and knowing she is a Dominator has created a win-win-win situation. A win for my wife (the house got finished as she wanted it); a win for me (not going to Baltimore) and a win for everyone else as her son would see the completed projects and remodeled home without all of the angst that used to accompany discussions between Jeannie and me.

Imagine if you truly "got" the people around you, and they "got" you.

As for the never-ending DIY project, we did finish the house at 11:30pm on the 18th, and I will NEVER do that again, but if I had not addressed the issue with her in the proper way, it never would have happened at all.

This was a landmark event for Jeannie and me, but immediately after our fight subsided, we sat down and talked about the way each of us was hardwired and finally developed a plan. This truly was our last big fight. Knowing why, and dealing with all the accompanying issues, has helped us create harmony in our relationship. I can honestly say that we don't clash anymore.

CHAPTER #18

Getting Me and Getting You

The following analyses will help you better understand yourself and those around you.

WHAT IS MY HARD WIRING?

Please use the following list to determine your orientation on the 4 key channels discussed. This is not a scientific test, but an easy way to determine your natural orientations. Once you do this self test, go to the next section and complete one on someone you know. Use the Quick interaction Guide in Chapter 19 to keep the information useful at all times!

Note: This is not to be used for hiring, but as a guide to improve interactions with others in your environment! Please be honest and sincere when completing.

Read through the following statements by section and circle the number that corresponds most closely to who you are. The scale is:

5 — Always applies to me
4 — Applies frequently to me
3 — Applies some of the time
2 — Rarely applies to me
1 — Never applies to me

Section 1: Self Evaluation DOMINATOR or ACCOMMODATOR?					
Question	Always Applies <-> Never Applies				
1) My ideas are the best ideas.	5	4	3	2	1
2) I like the best idea always.	5	4	3	2	1
3) Face-to-face conflict is exciting to me.	5	4	3	2	1
4) Being told no to something I want to do motivates me.	5	4	3	2	1
5) Accommodation is best when dealing with others.	5	4	3	2	1

Section 2: Self Evaluation EXTERNAL THINKER or INTERNAL THINKER?					
Question	Always Applies <-> Never Applies				
6) Face-to-face people interaction energizes me.	5	4	3	2	1
7) I come up with my best solution after alone time to think.	5	4	3	2	1
8) I like to figure things out for myself.	5	4	3	2	1
9) I repeat myself when I do not get a verbal response.	5	4	3	2	1
10) I ask for help when faced with a problem or situation.	5	4	3	2	1

Section 3: Self Evaluation HIGH PRESSURE OPERATOR *or* LOW PRESSURE OPERATOR?					
Question	Always Applies <-> Never Applies				
11) There are always too many things on my plate.	5	4	3	2	1
12) I make a checklist, but never follow it.	5	4	3	2	1
13) More pressure, more productivity for me.	5	4	3	2	1
14) I like doing things in a sequential manner — finishing one before going onto the next.	5	4	3	2	1
15) I have a short fuse.	5	4	3	2	1

Section 4: Self Evaluation PROOFER *or* BULLET POINTER?					
Question	Always Applies <-> Never Applies				
16) Give me serious proof on a new idea or concept	5	4	3	2	1
17) My decision making style is cautious.	5	4	3	2	1
18) The more details, the better for me.	5	4	3	2	1
19) Rules are to be followed.	5	4	3	2	1
20) I never break the rules, but do bend them frequently.	5	4	3	2	1.

SELF EVALUATION SCORING SHEET
FOR ME

This is how it works:

1) Go back to your test and look at your answer, which is to the right of the statement below and in the shaded area.
2) The corresponding point total is below the answer you circled — bold face in the un-shaded area.
3) Circle the point total in the un-shaded area and add up the points for each section.
4) The chart following this will reveal your natural tendencies or natural style.

Section 1: Scoring Sheet for Me
DOMINATOR or ACCOMMODATOR?

Question	Always Applies <-> Never Applies				
1) My ideas are the best ideas.	5	4	3	2	1
	5	4	3	2	1
2) I like the best idea always.	5	4	3	2	1
	1	2	3	4	5
3) Face-to-face conflict is exciting to me.	5	4	3	2	1
	5	4	3	2	1
4) Being told no to something I want to do motivates me.	5	4	3	2	1
	5	4	3	2	1
5) Accommodation is best when dealing with others.	5	4	3	2	1
	1	2	3	4	5
Point Total: _____					

Section 2: Scoring Sheet for Me
EXTERNAL THINKER or INTERNAL THINKER?

Question	Always Applies <-> Never Applies				
6) Face-to-face people interaction energizes me.	5	4	3	2	1
	5	4	3	2	1
7) I come up with my best solution after alone time to think.	5	4	3	2	1
	1	2	3	4	5
8) I like to figure things out for myself.	5	4	3	2	1
	1	2	3	4	5
9) I repeat myself when I do not get a verbal response.	5	4	3	2	1
	5	4	3	2	1
10) I ask for help when faced with a problem or situation.	5	4	3	2	1
	5	4	3	2	1
	Point Total: _____				

Section 3: Scoring Sheet for Me
HIGH PRESSURE OPERATOR or LOW PRESSURE OPERATOR?

Question	Always Applies <-> Never Applies				
11) There are always too many things on my plate.	5	4	3	2	1
	5	4	3	2	1
12) I make a checklist, but never follow it.	5	4	3	2	1
	5	4	3	2	1
13) More pressure, more productivity for me.	5	4	3	2	1
	5	4	3	2	1
14) I like doing things in a sequential manner — finishing one before going onto the next.	5	4	3	2	1
	1	2	3	4	5
15) I have a short fuse.	5	4	3	2	1
	5	4	3	2	1
	Point Total: _____				

Section 4: Scoring Sheet for Me PROOFER *or* BULLET POINTER?					
Question	Always Applies <-> Never Applies				
16) Give me serious proof on a new idea or concept.	5	4	3	2	1
	5	4	3	2	1
17) My decision making style is cautious.	5	4	3	2	1
	5	4	3	2	1
18) The more details, the better for me.	5	4	3	2	1
	5	4	3	2	1
19) Rules are to be followed.	5	4	3	2	1
	5	4	3	2	1
20) I never break the rules, but do bend them frequently.	5	4	3	2	1
	1	2	3	4	5
Point Total: _____					

116

SCORING ME — SECTION 1: ACCOMMODATOR OR DOMINATOR	
Score	Meaning
5-9	The Ultimate Teamer/Accommodator
10-14	Pretty much the team player
15-19	More dominator than teamer, but plays well with others
20-25	The Ultimate Dominator

SCORING ME — SECTION 2: INTERNAL OR EXTERNAL THINKER/COMMUNICATOR	
Score	Meaning
5-9	Very internal thinker and communicator
10-14	Comfortable verbal communicator, but likes alone time
15-19	More verbal than internal
20-25	Very external thinker and communicator

SCORING ME — SECTION 3: LOW OR HIGH PRESSURE OPERATOR	
Score	Meaning
5-9	Low Pressure Operator
10-14	Some pressure is okay; but keep it limited
15-19	Give me some pressure, don't overdo it!
20-25	High pressure Operator

SCORING ME — SECTION 4: BULLET POINTER OR PROOFER	
Score	Meaning
5-9	Basic and critical summary points
10-14	Bullet points plus basics, with some substantiating data
15-19	I want proof, just not the whole encyclopedia
20-25	Need lots and lots of data, information and proof

WHAT IS _____'S HARD WIRING?

Print copies of this form, fill in the name of the person you are trying to better understand, and go through the statements below. Circle the number that corresponds most closely to who they are.

5 — Always applies to them
4 — Applies frequently to them
3 — Applies some of the time
2 — Rarely applies to them
1 — Never applies to them

Section 1: Evaluation of _____ DOMINATOR or ACCOMMODATOR?					
Question	Always Applies <-> Never Applies				
1) Their ideas are the best ideas.	5	4	3	2	1
2) They like the best idea always.	5	4	3	2	1
3) Face-to-face conflict is exciting to them.	5	4	3	2	1
4) Being told no to something they want to do motivates them.	5	4	3	2	1
5) They are accommodating when dealing with others.	5	4	3	2	1

Section 2: Evaluation of _____ EXTERNAL THINKER or INTERNAL THINKER?					
Question	Always Applies <-> Never Applies				
6) Face-to-face people interaction energizes them.	5	4	3	2	1
7) They come up with their best solution after alone time to think.	5	4	3	2	1
8) They like to figure things out on their own.	5	4	3	2	1
9) They repeat themselves when they do not get a verbal response.	5	4	3	2	1
10) They ask for help when faced with a problem or situation.	5	4	3	2	1

Section 3: Evaluation of _____ HIGH PRESSURE OPERATOR *or* LOW PRESSURE OPERATOR?					
Question	Always Applies <-> Never Applies				
11) There are always too many things on their plate.	5	4	3	2	1
12) They make checklists, but never follow them.	5	4	3	2	1
13) More pressure, more productivity for them.	5	4	3	2	1
14) They like doing things in a sequential manner — finishing one before going onto the next.	5	4	3	2	1
15) They have a short fuse.	5	4	3	2	1

Section 4: Evaluation of _____ PROOFER *or* BULLET POINTER?					
Question	Always Applies <-> Never Applies				
16) Give them serious proof on a new idea or concept	5	4	3	2	1
17) Their decision making style is cautious.	5	4	3	2	1
18) The more details, the better for them.	5	4	3	2	1
19) They believe rules are to be followed.	5	4	3	2	1
20) They never break the rules, but do bend them frequently.	5	4	3	2	1

EVALUATION SCORING SHEET FOR OTHERS

This is how it works:

1) Go back to their test and look at your answer, which is to the right of the statement below and in the shaded area.

2) The corresponding point total is below the answer you circled — bold face in the un-shaded area.

3) Circle the point total in the un-shaded area and add up the points for each section.

4) The chart following this will reveal their natural tendencies or their natural style.

Section 1: Scoring Sheet for _____					
DOMINATOR or ACCOMMODATOR?					
Question	Always Applies <-> Never Applies				
1) Their ideas are the best ideas.	5	4	3	2	1
	5	**4**	**3**	**2**	**1**
2) They like the best idea always.	5	4	3	2	1
	1	**2**	**3**	**4**	**5**
3) Face-to-face conflict is exciting to them.	5	4	3	2	1
	5	**4**	**3**	**2**	**1**
4) Being told no to something they want to do motivates them.	5	4	3	2	1
	5	**4**	**3**	**2**	**1**
5) They are accommodating when dealing with others.	5	4	3	2	1
	1	**2**	**3**	**4**	**5**
Point Total: _____					

Section 2: Scoring Sheet for _____
EXTERNAL THINKER *or* **INTERNAL THINKER?**

Question	Always Applies <-> Never Applies				
6) Face-to-face people interaction energizes them.	5	4	3	2	1
	5	4	3	2	1
7) They come up with their best solution after alone time to think.	5	4	3	2	1
	1	2	3	4	5
8) They like to figure things out on their own.	5	4	3	2	1
	1	2	3	4	5
9) They repeat themselves when they do not get a verbal response.	5	4	3	2	1
	5	4	3	2	1
10) They ask for help when faced with a problem or situation.	5	4	3	2	1
	5	4	3	2	1
Point Total: _____					

Section 3: Scoring Sheet for _____
HIGH PRESSURE OPERATOR *or* **LOW PRESSURE OPERATOR?**

Question	Always Applies <-> Never Applies				
11) There are always too many things on their plate.	5	4	3	2	1
	5	4	3	2	1
12) They make checklists, but never follow them.	5	4	3	2	1
	5	4	3	2	1
13) More pressure, more productivity for them.	5	4	3	2	1
	5	4	3	2	1
14) They like doing things in a sequential manner — finishing one before going onto the next.	5	4	3	2	1
	1	2	3	4	5
15) They have a short fuse.	5	4	3	2	1
	5	4	3	2	1
Point Total: _____					

Section 4: Scoring Sheet for _____ PROOFER *or* BULLET POINTER?					
Question	Always Applies <-> Never Applies				
16) Give them serious proof on a new idea or concept.	5	4	3	2	1
	5	4	3	2	1
17) Their decision making style is cautious.	5	4	3	2	1
	5	4	3	2	1
18) The more details, the better for them.	5	4	3	2	1
	5	4	3	2	1
19) They believe rules are to be followed.	5	4	3	2	1
	5	4	3	2	1
20) They never break the rules, but do bend them frequently.	5	4	3	2	1
	1	2	3	4	5
Point Total: _____					

SCORING OTHERS — SECTION 1: ACCOMMODATOR OR DOMINATOR	
Score	Meaning
5-9	The Ultimate Teamer/Accommodator
10-14	Pretty much the team player
15-19	More dominator than teamer, but plays well with others
20-25	The Ultimate Dominator

SCORING OTHERS — SECTION 2: INTERNAL OR EXTERNAL THINKER/COMMUNICATOR	
Score	Meaning
5-9	Very internal thinker and communicator
10-14	Comfortable verbal communicator, but likes alone time
15-19	More verbal than internal
20-25	Very external thinker and communicator

SCORING OTHERS — SECTION 3: LOW OR HIGH PRESSURE OPERATOR	
Score	Meaning
5-9	Low Pressure Operator
10-14	Some pressure is okay; but keep it limited
15-19	Give them some pressure, don't overdo it!
20-25	High pressure Operator

SCORING OTHERS — SECTION 4: BULLET POINTER OR PROOFER	
Score	Meaning
5-9	Basic and critical summary points
10-14	Bullet points plus basics, with some substantiating data
15-19	They want proof, just not the whole encyclopedia
20-25	Need lots and lots of data, information and proof

CHAPTER #19

Quick Interaction Guide

DOMINANCE (IDEA FLOW)	
ACCOMMODATOR:	**DOMINATOR:**
· Wants the idea that best benefits the team or group · Contributes ideas best when in a "conflict free" environment · Likes to hear all of the options for the "best" idea	· Wants to implement their idea or have input on how the idea is executed · Let them put their thumbprint on the idea by asking: "How do you think we should proceed?" · Needs elements of control in their environment

COMMUNICATION

INTERNAL THINKER:	EXTERNAL THINKER:
· Does best with time to "Think" issues through · Won't give response until thought process is complete (blank stare or silence)	· Does best with time to "Verbalize" issues through · Wants response from the other party

PRESSURE / SPEED OF DECISION MAKING

LOW PRESSURE OPERATOR:	HIGH PRESSURE OPERATOR:
· Wants to make "deliberate" decision · Pressure will slow decision making process · Likes to finish one thing before moving onto the next · Has a longer fuse	· Wants to make "quick" decision · Accepts making "pressure" decisions · Piles a lot on their plates · Has a shorter fuse

DECISION MAKING INFORMATION

BULLET POINTER:	PROOFER:
· Wants the "summary sheet" or "bullet point" information · Tends to block out excessive information or detail · Comfortable making a risk decision	· Wants details or "proof" to validate statements · Statements with examples create proof · Wants to reduce chance of failure in decision making

ABOUT THE AUTHOR

James "Jay" Hawreluk has a BBA in Business Management from the University of Michigan and an MBA from the University of Detroit. From his involvement in a youth organization, to his first full time position at a bank, as a business owner and involved in sales and consulting, people have always fascinated him. Over the years, Jay has tried to figure people out and address the issue of why they do the things they do. This culminated when he become a Predictive Index® Consultant in late 2000 and for over 10 years worked with all size organizations to provide recruiting, hiring, management, team building and strategic planning expertise. The PI® is a drive-based instrument that reveals how people are best motivated, communicate, work and make decisions.

As a former CEO, Jay has years of hands on experience in dealing with the many complex issues that occur in today's business environment. After orchestrating the buy out of his company in the early 1990's, Jay has continued to work with executives of small to Fortune 500 companies offering realistic and attainable solutions to the challenges of our dynamic business world. The hallmark of Jay's career has been his ability to consistently deliver new approaches that generate quality results to his clientele at the highest levels of customer satisfaction. These efforts have resulted in Jay being recognized for multiple years as a "Worldwide Top Performing" Predictive Index® Consultant.

The information Jay has acquired over many years of working with companies is now available to all in his new book — *Unraveling the Mystery of People* — which now enables all people to improve their relationships, job satisfaction and overall life enjoyment!

Jay's educational and entertaining presentation style has lead to speaking engagements with Vistage (an association of Chief Executive Officers), Michigan Association of Medical Assistants, Society of Human Resource Managers, Precision Machining Parts Association National Convention, Petro Canada America National Convention and the IFDA National Convention. He is a proud member of the National Speakers Association.

Predictive Index® is a registered trademark of Praendex or its subsidiaries in the United States and other countries.

Unraveling the Mystery of People is an independent publication and is not affiliated with, nor has it been authorized, sponsored, or otherwise approved by PI Worldwide® or Praendex.

www.JayHaw.com